Bricks for Breakfast

Bricks for Breakfast

A Story of Healing
Through Love and Fitness

Meredith Thornton

with Linda Tatro Herzer

Meredith Thornton
Springdale, Arkansas

Bricks for Breakfast: A Story of Healing Through Love and Fit-
ness/Meredith Thornton with Linda Tatro Herzer
ISBN: 979-8-218-18533-6
ISBN: (e-book) 979-8-218-18534-3

I dedicate this book to my biggest fan . . . my husband.
Through your love and support I found my way to healing
which allowed me to chase my dream of becoming an Ironman.

CONTENTS

Introduction   9
PART I: BUILDING A FOUNDATION

1: My First Battle   14

2: My Childhood Monster   18

3: Childhood Violence and Coping Mechanisms   23

4: Reflections on My Biological Parents   33

PART II: MY TEEN YEARS

5: The Move   43

6: The House from Hell   49

7: My First Job   55

8: My First Love   60

9: My High School Career   65

10: Escaping   72

PART III: MY ROARING TWENTIES

11: Girls Just Wanna Have Fun   78

12: The Wreck   86

13: Humiliation and Degradation   96

PART IV: A DECADE OF DISASTROUS MARRIAGES

14: The Controller   118

15: A Tragic Ending   127

16: My Father, the Funeral, and the Investigation   142

17: Alcoholic #2 Becomes Husband #3   152

PART V: MY FORTIES—STORIES OF HEALING

18: My Biggest Fan   163

19: First Steps to Healing   173

20: Hoffman   181

PART VI: THE ROAD TO HEALING THROUGH FITNESS

21: Finding My Passion   193

22: The Diagnosis   203

23: Treatments and Triathlon   210

24: Outside my Comfort Zone   223

25: Silver Linings   230

26: Chasing My Dreams   237

27: What it Takes   241

28: My First Ironman 140.6   248

Epilogue   266

Introduction

I wasn't born tattered. I wasn't born to question whether I was enough or whether I deserved to breathe the air around me. I wasn't born to hate my body and torment myself over every scar and pound. I certainly wasn't born to accept abuse from another's hand or to let the demeaning words they spoke penetrate and destroy the very idea of my self-worth. I was *taught* to believe that I was worthless, undeserving, incapable, and other lies about myself. As a child, I was handed these bricks which formed the foundation of this version of reality that I accepted throughout my life.... until I learned to stop letting it be my reality.

While adopting my new reality, a passion for the sport of triathlon ignited within me. In this community, it's common to hear someone say, "I had bricks for breakfast." This means that they engaged in a particular type of workout that day. Their workout occurred early in the morning, before *breakfast,* and it included a *brick*, the back-to-back completion of two of the three disciplines of a triathlon. The most common is the bike-to-run brick. Triathletes have to practice running immediately after biking because our legs actually feel like bricks when we start out on the run—hence the term "bricks" to describe this type of workout. To be competitive, we must experience this brick sensation numerous times in order to understand and be able to work with it. During my very first attempt at a bike-to-run brick workout, I felt like a drunken Gumby!

I chose the phrase "bricks for breakfast" as the title of this book to celebrate the path of healing through fitness that I am now traveling. Despite what my abusers told me, the truth is, I am strong. I can do hard things. And one of the ways I demonstrate this is by having "bricks for breakfast".

I also chose this phrase to honor the journey I have traveled to get to this point. In my own thinking, I use the word "bricks" to describe the messages I received and used to build the foundation of my self-worth. In this metaphorical sense, a cracked or broken brick represents negative messaging, while a sturdy brick represents positive messages. In the same way that it's important for me to start each day by giving my body a healthy breakfast, when children are first starting out in life, it's important for them to be given strong, reliable bricks, that is, positive, healthy messaging about their self-worth. Unfortunately, this was not my experience.

Because I was given broken bricks in my childhood, messages of shame and unworthiness, for my first two decades as an adult, I found myself in one abusive relationship after another. I allowed more than one man to treat me like the worthless person I believed myself to be.

It wasn't until I was in my forties that I found my way to a Twelve-Step program and another type of healing program. Both helped me understand the dynamics of the cycle of violence I had been caught in and how I could break the cycle. Through these programs I encountered healthy messaging, acquired the necessary tools to change, rewired the way I thought about myself, and found my voice. And once I did—once I started down that journey of challenging myself, of pushing my limits, of staring fear in the face—that's when my passion for triathlon burst forth. My newly found self-love ignited this fire that had been smoldering deep within me all these years.

Even while fighting breast cancer, my passion for triathlon burned so hot that I was determined to train, determined to compete, determined to achieve my goals and complete my first half Ironman. As I would leave my radiation treatments to go work out as best I could, the women who were receiving treatments with me would tell me how inspired they were by my passion and commitment. Their words of encouragement planted a seed within me, the thought that maybe one day I could share my story to inspire others.

That seed was nurtured by the few who know what it's taken for me to overcome the abuse from my childhood and the domestic violence I experienced as an adult. They have encouraged me to tell my stories, believing my experiences could empower others.

Author Alex Elle writes, *"You're not a victim for sharing your story. You are a survivor setting the world on fire with your truth. And you never know who needs your light, your warmth, and raging courage."*

So here they are, a lifetime of stories about the survival of the human spirit and the power of healing through love and fitness. May they inspire you to find your passion, to allow yourself to dream, to have the self-love and confidence to try, and in trying, to accomplish great things. May they ignite within you the same deep knowing that I now have—that I am unstoppable and I am unbreakable.

PART ONE

BUILDING A FOUNDATION

ONE

My First Battle

"The human spirit is stronger
than anything that can happen to it."

C. C Scott

I was two years old the first time I beat death.

It was 1973. President Nixon was sworn in for his second term. Elvis Presley held a concert in Hawaii that was watched by more people than the Apollo moon landing. The World Trade Center officially opened in New York City. Even more important to my story was the fact that the last United States soldier left Vietnam on March 29, 1973.

My mother was still married to my birth father who was serving a tour in Vietnam. This left my mother to care for myself and my older brother on her own. I had fallen ill with something that initially manifested as flu-like symptoms. Mom told me the story of how she took me to the Oakland Naval Hospital twice, because I was not improving. Both times, the doctors simply told her I had the flu, and then sent us away.

When I became lethargic with fever, my maternal grandfather insisted on accompanying my mom to the hospital for yet a third visit. He had seen enough. He was stepping in to take over. My grandpa was not going to accept anything less from the doctor than a full work up on me. He insisted I had something more serious than the flu. My grandpa's persistence paid off. This time, the doctors took my illness more seriously. They conducted a spinal tap and the test results showed I had spinal meningitis.

Spinal meningitis is an infection of the fluid and the membranes around the brain and spinal cord. If left untreated it can cause brain damage in a matter of hours. It can be fatal in as quickly as twenty-four hours. So how did I survive for days at home without this infection killing me? How did I not end up with brain damage or other disabilities due to the delay in treatment? I believe this was the first time my guardian angel came to my rescue.

Now, I recognize that not everyone believes in angels, but I do. Woven in with all the suffering and abuse I've experienced throughout my life are numerous incidents where I have survived for no other reason that I can see except that I had a guardian angel whose sole job was to keep me alive and breathing. In the past, I always thought this to be the waste of a good angel's time and energy. I did not feel like I ever deserved to be spared or to take up space on this planet. I never understood why I was supposed to be alive. Now I think I have been spared over and over because maybe my story can help other people; maybe it will even save a life. Perhaps that's my purpose on this earth and why I am still here.

Regardless of the how and the why of my continued existence, by the time my illness was diagnosed correctly, I had deteriorated to a very dangerous point. The doctor had no choice but to admit me to the hospital where I stayed for over a week.

During that week, my temperature elevated to 105 degrees. The doctor called my mom and instructed her to come up to the hospital immediately because there were things they needed to discuss. A fever of 105 degrees is considered a medical emergency. To put it in perspective, a temperature over 107.6 can cause brain damage. It was apparent that I was teetering on the brink of survival. I could not afford to get any worse. My little body had just about reached its limits, and decisions had to be made about my care.

As a mother now myself, I cannot image the worry, terror, and fear my mom must have experienced while the doctor walked her through the situation, her options, and the repercussions if she made the wrong decision. At that very moment, she had to make an impossible decision that no mother should ever have to make.

The doctor gave her two options. Option One: they could administer a medicine that would be effective in fighting the virus but had a 50 percent chance of causing deafness. Option Two: they could continue down the road of the antibiotics I was currently on and see if my body could fight off the infection. Both options were risky. The latter could have killed me. There were also risks of long-term complications such as seizures, loss of vision, brain damage and, in rare cases, even loss of limbs. My mom decided I was strong. She decided to give me time to fight off the illness without the risk of becoming deaf.

The miracle came a couple days later when I began to turn a corner. Come to find out, I was indeed strong enough to fight that battle.

I write about this first struggle with death from my mother's memories, as I do not have any of my own that reach that far back into childhood. When I decided to tell my story, I knew I would have to rely on my mom to bridge many gaps for me. During my first conversation with her about these events, it dawned on me that, in over forty years, we had never once discussed the two major childhood illnesses I survived. Based on what I learned from that talk, I realized that our lives had been so chaotic and so toxic that we never had "normal" conversations. The memories of most of what we had endured together were shoved deep down inside us. They just didn't get discussed. If you don't talk about it, it doesn't exist, and everything is fine. That's how we operated as a family. That's how we functioned—or malfunctioned, to be more accurate.

When I was forty-nine, my mom shared this whole story of my battle with spinal meningitis with me. I was astounded at how strong I was—even at such a young age. A sense of pride filled me as she spoke about my strength and resilience and how I had beaten the Grim Reaper right out of the gate. I was obviously unaware, as a toddler, of just how important this first experience would be for me; how this strength and resilience would serve me later in life; how it would save my life repeatedly. I had to fight for my right to breathe air from this point on. Maybe that's why God, or the universe, or my guardian angel placed me in this position at such an early age: to condition me, to train me, to acclimate me to fight, to survive.

TWO

My Childhood Monster

"Only the weakest takes advantage
of a child's defenselessness."

quotesempire.com

My earliest childhood memory is of my mother and stepfather's wedding. I was wearing a pretty dress and my hair was done in ribbons and curls. I was bursting with optimism and happiness! My four-year-old self was experiencing what all little girls should be at that age. I gleefully chased other children around a pool, oblivious to the path that had now been laid out for me by my mother, unaware of how it would affect the rest of my life. I had no way of knowing that this was the last time I would be so carefree. I didn't know that I was now on my way to the nightmare that would be my life for the next thirteen years.

* * * * * * * * * *

Many children have invisible monsters hiding under their beds or in their closets. My childhood monster was not only visible, but standing six foot seven, he towered over me and everyone else.

Norman, my mother's new husband and my new monster, used his physical build to threaten and drive fear into my family. (All names have been changed except that of my current husband.) He knew that just his size alone was intimidating to most people. The full beard that hid part of his face somehow made him feel even scarier to me, especially when he was angry. I could often feel the heat of his breath as he got right in my face to yell at me. All these things, combined with the crazy-eyed look he got when he lost control, made Norman downright terrifying. We never knew if he was going to strike us or not, but he always looked like he wanted to end our lives.

Norman had something that caused his moods to be either euphoric or off-the-rails mad. You would think that, when he was in a good mood, we could all have a moment of peace and breathe a little easier. But we couldn't. When Norman was in a good mood, it was almost worse for us. When he was in a happy state, we knew it was just a matter of time before he crashed. My childhood monster was a ticking time bomb . . . Every. Single. Day.

Surgery and Scars

At the age of five, my biggest worry should have been whether or not it was going to rain so I could go outside and play. Instead, I was dealing with Norman and another illness. I had frequent fevers and tummy aches, along with kidney and bladder infections. I would wet my bed and wake up from naps wringing wet with sweat. Norman berated me for my bed-wetting and accused me of lying about being sick. He forced me to go to school, even though I was not feeling well. One day, I remember crying as I tried to get dressed. I felt so poorly I could barely get my clothes on.

The doctors finally discovered that my left kidney was malformed, and that the Ureter, the tube attached to it, was twisted. They said the only way to correct the malformation of my kidney was to remove half of it and then fix the Ureter. This meant surgery and hospitalization.

I remember only three things from my stay in the hospital. First, Norman became irate when I communicated that I only wanted to see my grandpa. My maternal grandpa was the only loving father figure I had, so as a child, I was very attached to him. My mom described my grandpa as emotionally unattached and withholding when she was a child, but as a granddaughter with her grandpa, I was fortunate to have a different experience.

My second memory is that my older brother was not allowed into my hospital room during one of my family's visits. He had a cold and I could not risk getting it. Finally, I remember celebrating the day of my sixth birthday in the hospital. The staff made me my very favorite meal as a kid: a grilled cheese sandwich and a chocolate shake. They also made some sort of whipped cream cake. Unfortunately, I did not feel like eating any of it because the pain meds I was on seriously diminished my appetite.

While I don't remember everything that occurred in the hospital, I have vivid memories of what happened when I got home. My grandparents had bought me a new bed for my birthday! I was so happy to discover that canopy bed with a pink gingham design all set up in my room! In my little mind, it looked like it came straight out of a fairytale. It looked like something a princess would sleep in, with its ruffles and matching sheets and blanket. The thought that I had it in my bedroom, and that I was the one who was going to sleep in it, made me feel very special. One of my best childhood memories is the pure joy I felt over something so simple as my new canopy bed.

As with any major surgery, I was supposed to rest at home for several weeks before resuming my regular activities, like going to school. My mom had recently had another baby, so with me on bedrest and a new infant to care for, she hired a babysitter to help. One day, my being home set Norman off into one of his angry fits. Apparently, he thought I had recovered enough and was perfectly fine to get back to my normal routine. I remember the startled look on the babysitter's face, like she could not believe what she was seeing, as Norman screamed at me because I was not in school. My mom was at work, so I had no one there to intervene or diffuse the situation. The new babysitter reluctantly conceded to his wishes. She helped me get dressed and sent me on my way. We lived within walking distance of my elementary school, so I had to walk alone. I think the sitter would have come with me if she hadn't had to stay home and care for my baby brother. I cried the entire way. My teacher was surprised when I walked through the classroom door, which also let me know that I was not ready to go back when I did.

That babysitter Mom hired didn't stay with us long. She was afraid of my stepfather, and he quickly ran her off. I was jealous of her ability to escape my home while I had to stay there and endure Norman's instability.

My kidney surgery left a huge scar that wrapped around the entire left side of my body. Even at a young age, I was very self-conscious about that scar. It became a physical representation of the emotional scarring occurring inside me.

My monster perpetuated the idea that I needed to feel ashamed of my scar. Norman would put me on display for others to view, like I was some sort of freak show. I did not want to show off my scar and would try to refuse. I always broke down in tears when he made me do it anyway. I didn't want to be an anomaly. What I needed was to be told that scars are nothing to be ashamed of. I needed to be told that my scars were beautiful because they show that I beat whatever it was that tried to take me down. The message that should have been instilled in me was that I should be proud of my scar because it proves I am a warrior, a princess warrior. That would have made all the difference in the world. Instead, I was mocked, and ogled, and put on display, as if there was something wrong with me.

Through these shaming experiences with my scar, Norman gave me the first of many "gifts." This gift was broken bricks that built my faulty foundation of shame, low self-worth, and the belief that I was not enough. This unsteady foundation gave rise to distorted views of myself, which led to harmful views of men, love, and relationships. As a young child, I didn't have the ability to refuse this false reality Norman created for me. My brain became programmed with negativity that, to this day, I still have to work to overcome. You could say it was quite the gift . . . a gift that keeps on giving. Sadly, Norman was a giver like that.

THREE

Childhood Violence and Coping Mechanisms

*"The greater a child's terror, and the earlier it is experienced,
the harder it becomes to develop a strong
and healthy sense of self."*
Nathaniel Branden

Norman was very proud of his six-foot-seven stature, and he liked to use force even outside the home. One night, my mom came home from work upset. She told my stepfather that some guys in a car had given her trouble while she was driving home. They had turned off into the apartment complex across the street from us. Norman made her get in the car with him and go point out the vehicle. They drove around the complex until she spotted the car. Norman got out and bashed it with a tire iron. He came home laughing, almost giddy, with blood on his hands. He must have cut himself or gotten physical with one of the men. I'm not sure which. The point is, he enjoyed it. The violence gave Norman some sort of high. He came back elated and bragged on himself while he told us the story.

As an adult, I now realize that Norman was just continuing the cycle of violence he grew up with. Norman's mother was an alcoholic and his father was just cruel and abusive. I'll never know exactly what caused Norman to be so violent. There may have been mental illness in the family that went undiagnosed, or maybe it was just learned behavior for Norman. What I have learned is that violence is a common systemic issue that occurs within a broken family unit when the family system is left in-tact. Sadly, no one broke that cycle of violence for Norman as a child. I do feel sorry for all he endured as a kid. However, I don't feel sorry for him as an adult, because Norman chose to perpetuate that cycle within his own family unit. I use the word "chose" because violence is a choice. I chose to break the cycle for my family, as did my brothers. And it wasn't like Norman had no control over his violent actions. I know this because, while he was physically abusive to my older brother and myself—his stepchildren—he never laid a hand on my younger brother, who was his own biological child.

Norman was fond of a technique I call "violence in exchange for obedience." He frequently punched holes in the walls, threw whatever was closest to him, or broke our personal belongings and our most treasured toys. Anything for shock and awe; anything to get our attention and to remind us who was the dominant one in the household. The more something meant to us, the bigger the target it became for destruction or confiscation.

The one incident I remember the most, the one I cannot shake, even after all this time, is the day he tore my older brother's room apart. I don't remember what my brother had done that angered Norman, but nothing he could have done deserved the irrational and violent reaction he received. Entering the room, Norman broke all the toy models my brother had spent hours making. He smashed them into little bits and pieces.

Back in the '80s, toy models came in a box with plastic sheets of model car pieces that had to be manually separated from each sheet. From there, each piece was painted by hand. When those dried, they were glued together. This was a process that took days and was painstakingly detailed. I think working on his models was a means of escape for my brother. He certainly enjoyed getting lost in the construction of those vehicles.

These model cars were my brother's prized possessions. They were displayed proudly on shelves in his room, like personal medals of achievement. Watching Norman destroy those models was one of the most heartbreaking scenes I have ever witnessed. I still tear up whenever I remember the look on my brother's face as it happened.

Even family vacations were not exempt from Norman's violence. The trips always began with anticipation and excitement, with the sense that we were a "normal" family. Norman would start out on one of his highs, but this put me on edge because I knew the crash was coming. The lows always hit, and it was usually something minor that set him off or nothing at all. We never knew. The vacations would always result in tears, temper tantrums, name calling, and broken shit. It was like vacationing with a six-foot-seven toddler who always needed a nap.

I remember one trip in particular, when we went camping by a lake. My brothers and I were playing in the water on floatable rafts, and we started squabbling, as siblings will. Norman heard us from onshore and blew up. He turned over all the breakfast dishes and ruined our meal. I vividly recall him stamping out the open fire we had been cooking over. He made sure none of us could finish our food as punishment for the bickering.

The Twins

Norman's violent acts did not begin with our family. My monster had started this pattern of behavior when he married his first wife, with whom he had fraternal twin boys. Sometimes, these stepbrothers would come visit us during the summer. Since they lived in Nevada and we were in California, these are about the only times we saw them. When these stepbrothers came to visit, they received the same harsh treatment as everyone else in the house—with the exception of my younger brother—so eventually, they quit coming at all. Just like our babysitter, they also had a choice, but I was still forced to stay.

Norman's twins grew to be quite large and were as big, or bigger than their dad. When they came to visit the summer I was thirteen, they were huge . . . teenagers as large as he was. One of them had gotten in trouble for something, and Norman wasted no time stripping off his belt. These punishments were not always private events, so it was not uncommon for the rest of us to have to witness someone getting whipped. This day though . . . on this day, things didn't go quite as planned for our monster. As he tried to take a belt to his son, that man-child grabbed the belt from his dad and stared him down like he was going to eat his face. The look on Norman's face was both of shock and surprise. It was the most amazing thing I had ever seen! Inside, I was cheering for my stepbrother. He was like a superhero to me that day. And that was it. That was the end of their visits.

I realized then that Monster only preyed on those who were weaker than he was, or who were afraid of him. I vowed right then and there that one day, when I was bigger, I would also stand up to him. Witnessing that it could be done, that it was possible, gave me hope that, someday soon, I would stand up for myself as a human being. I so desperately wanted to be brave like that. I wanted to be able to force a look of shock and surprise on Norman's face. I eventually did, but it took several more years for me to build up the courage to do so.

Shamed in Puberty

When I was twelve, my body began to develop as I hit puberty. I felt like a late bloomer, seeing as my friends had already been wearing bras for at least a year. As I've shared earlier, I developed body image issues at the age of six, thanks to Norman shaming me because of the large scar from my kidney surgery. Feeling like an underachiever in the development department exacerbated these issues. Even girls with all the self-assurance in the world still find themselves losing some of that confidence as their bodies begin to change. Boys make fun of you if you are flat-chested or if you develop too early. That does not even include adding the horror of the monthly period into the mix! This stage in a teenage girl's life is already emotional, confusing, and embarrassing to navigate, but my challenges were compounded by the fact that something about me hitting puberty did not sit well with Norman.

It's not that he was any more hateful, or that he acted out more than usual. But it felt like the focal point had shifted. Now, when Norman hit me with his belt, he made sure to strike me in places where he knew I would cover up the bruises so they wouldn't show. This was never a focus before. He used to just randomly swing and make contact wherever the leather fell. But after entering puberty, I remember him laughing as he hit my legs with his belt, saying, "You won't wear shorts for a week now." And he was right. I didn't wear shorts until the bruises were completely gone, even though it was the middle of summer.

Swimsuits became another focus for shaming and ridicule. I would not wear a bikini due to the scar from my kidney surgery, so my swimsuits were always one-piece suits. I never wore the midriff tops that had become so popular because my scar showed if I raised my arms. I certainly wasn't flaunting my new curves, but for some reason, Norman would still shame me for wearing a simple, tasteful, one-piece suit.

I'll never forget what happened the day I wore my new turquoise swimsuit. It had a cute little cut-out in the front and back, so bits of my belly and back were exposed, but it was connected on the sides, so it covered most of my scar. I wanted to feel more grown up, as most of my friends sported bikinis, and I thought this suit was perfect! My mom had bought it for me, and I could not wait to wear it.

One weekend, our family went to a local beach. Norman spotted some teenage boys who must have been looking in my general direction. I was unaware of their attention, so I was completely caught off guard when Norman erupted. He demanded I put on a shirt and shouted that I was a "slut" and a "whore." I was mortified, embarrassed, and immediately ashamed of my beautiful new turquoise swimsuit with the cut-outs in the front and back.

These types of incidents were common for the next couple of years. Each one continued to fuel my body image insecurities and my sense of worthlessness.

What was it that threatened Norman to the point where he focused on these changes I was going through? I was growing out of childish things, so maybe that was the threat. The older I got, the less afraid I became, and the less I considered him my childhood monster. Maybe Norman understood that it was no longer fear, but humiliation, that was needed to keep me under his thumb.

More broken bricks being piled on to my already unstable foundation. More bad messaging. More self-hatred.

Coping Mechanisms

Like most children growing up in dysfunctional families, I developed various coping mechanisms to survive my monster's violence and the chaos of my homelife. As a young child, I sucked my thumb to manage my stress. I also chewed my fingernails. This was not the regular nibbling, but the kind of psychotic chewing that resulted in bloody fingertips. To this day, I still have a horrible habit of chewing my nails, and the skin around them, whenever I'm nervous or stressed.

Another coping mechanism I adopted was burying myself in the alternate realities of books and my own imagination. For a large part of my childhood, I would play out scenarios in my head or with my dolls where I had a different family dynamic. I even went so far as to pray, every single night, that my monster would die in a fiery car accident and not come home at all. He was a truck driver, so I figured that could be a real possibility. It's awful when I see this in print, but that's how badly I wanted my life to be different; that's how much I wanted my life to be "normal." I was a child who had been put in a position where I had to make up stories in my head to survive the reality of what was going on within the walls of my home.

My fear and stress consumed me. I could not get away from it even when I slept. I had night terrors that went on for years. These night terrors shared a common theme; there was always someone chasing me because they wanted to kill me. Whether it was a monster, a demon, or a popular character from a scary movie I had just watched, they all had the same mission. What classifies these dreams as night terrors versus just regular nightmares was the intensity of the dreams and the debilitating effect they had on me. They seemed so real to me that they were absolutely paralyzing. I was terrified to go to sleep. The sad part is, I was also terrified to stay awake. I just couldn't win!

My night terrors got so bad that I learned how to wake myself up from them. I had survival tactics I had learned to use during the day, and now I was forced to learn new strategies to get me through the night. The humorous part of this was that I saw this tactic in a movie, and the idea just stuck with me. I have no idea how I did it or learned to do it. I just know that I used to tell myself to wake up, and I could pull myself out of my night terror.

While most of my coping mechanisms were something I did,

one of them was something I stopped doing. As a kid, one of my favorite television shows was Grizzly Adams. The show was about an innocent fugitive that hid in the wilderness with a grizzly bear. This fugitive was gentle and kind, very much like the father I always wished I had. And he would always help those in need. I loved this show… until Grizzly Adam's beard and height began to physically remind me of Norman. My monster was like the Hyde version of Grizzly Adams. Once my mind made that association, it wasn't long before it made me too sad and too scared to watch that show, so I stopped watching it.

When I was discussing my childhood with my mom, she was the one who told me about the bed-wetting that occurred because of my malformed kidney, and how enraged Norman would get because I was wetting my bed at the age of five. I was surprised to learn of this because I had no recollection of these embarrassing and shameful episodes. I have heard that sometimes our brains block out certain traumatic events, so it seems this is another survival tactic I used without even realizing it.

As I got older, I tried to stay away from the house as much as possible. I continued this through my teen years, until I left home permanently when I was seventeen years old. I would spend as much time at friends' houses as I possibly could. It was nice to have a place to go where I could relax, even if just briefly. But I was also sad and jealous when I was in those households because I desperately wanted to be like my friends. I was also sad, and maybe even a little angry, that my friends took their "normal" environment for granted. They took for granted that, every day, they got to come home to a safe place, free from the toxic chaos that was my life. They did not realize that what they perceived as "boring" family conversations around the dinner table were so coveted by me. They did not know that some people were not lucky enough to have this. For all these reasons, witnessing these somewhat "normal" family units was a bitter-sweet experience for me. But since I still craved normality, I wedged myself in anywhere I could find a place.

Looking back over these coping mechanisms I developed in order to survive my monster, I realize that, ironically, some of them helped me later in life when I was faced with other abusers. *Maybe I should thank Norman for being my first teacher.*

FOUR

Reflections on My Biological Parents

*"To be in your children's memories tomorrow,
you have to be in their lives today."*

Barbara Johnson

The fundamental needs of a child are not complex. To survive, they must have their basic needs met: food, clothing, shelter and medical care. To thrive, they must have security, stability, consistency, emotional support, love, education, positive role models, and structure. My basic needs were met, and I survived, but I was not given the things I needed to thrive. All of those important things were absent from my life, or sporadic at best. From a young age, I was always searching for ways to meet these needs, as best as I could; trying to fill the voids. I was always trying to change my narrative and find validation that I was indeed lovable, that I was worthy of my existence. That's why I constantly looked for my biological father. I hoped that he could be found and that he would fill in these gaps and help me rewrite my story.

My Biological Father

The only details I have about the few years my biological parents were married are that they wed in 1967 and divorced around 1973 or 1974. I also know that my father was absent for about half of their short marriage.

My father was not an abusive or cruel person. My parents were just young when they married and Dad was gone so much that they simply drifted apart and became strangers. My father was in the Navy and had been serving a tour in Vietnam. I can only imagine what horrors he saw there, and I try to tell myself that maybe this had something to do with his absence. At least in this scenario, I am not the reason he was gone. In this scenario, I am not the reason for his absence; I am not unlovable.

As a child trying to survive under the tyranny of my stepfather, I would frequently get lost in my head, daydreaming about another life. I would make up stories which all had fairy tale endings. In these stories I would find my absent father, and he would take me away to live with him. I would finally be the princess I dreamed about. He would tell me that he had been looking for me all these years; that he had no idea where me and my brother were. I went so far as to scour the phonebook and look up his name to try and narrow down the search. I remembered Mom saying once that she thought he may still be around in the Bay Area, my childhood home. But Dad had a common name and there were hundreds, if not thousands, of his name listed in the phone book. It was like finding a needle in a haystack. But I kept dreaming. In my mind, I would imagine that he made lots of money so when I did go live with him, I would have everything I ever wanted. My mom never knew of my fantasies, or that I would call people listed in the phone book to try and find him. I would hide that precious phone-book under my bed, or in my closet, or in my dresser drawers. It was my little secret. It gave me hope—until it didn't.

My fantasies were crushed the first time I met my biological father. Well, I didn't actually meet him; I simply caught a glimpse of him from my front door. It took just those few moments to de-stroy my dreams of living with him, of being rescued, of living a normal life.

I don't know how it happened that my dad was coming over, whether my mom insisted, or if he did so willingly. I also don't remember my exact age, but it was well before my pre-teen years. I just remember thinking I was going to be saved. My dad was coming over to take my brother and I out to eat, and I was certain that, from that moment on, our lives would change. I was certain I was either going to get to go live with him or, at the very least, see him on a regular basis. I just knew that if I could tell him about how cruel and violent my stepdad was that he would fight for us.

None of that took place. I didn't even get to go out to eat with my dad and brother.

When he showed up, he arrived in a vehicle that had only two seats. To say that I was devastated would be an understatement. My mom tried to console me by telling me I could go the next time. But there never was a "next time."

After that day, I never saw my dad again until I was twen-ty-seven years old. That's when my obsession with finding him, and the creation of the internet, finally enabled me to track him down. I actually flew back to California to try and reunite. During my visit, he did not elaborate in detail about the marriage with mom, or why he was not a part of my life growing up. I did not get the answers I wanted and needed to work towards finding closure with him. Shortly after that visit, when I asked my mom about his absence, I didn't get any real answers from her either. At the end of the day, the conclusion I've come to is that he just chose not to be around. He chose to not be a father. I'm sure he had his reasons, but I doubt I will ever know what those reasons were then—or what they continue to be to this day.

Another thing I learned from that visit left me feeling sad and unsettled, but mostly just downright livid! It turns out my dad had lived about an hour from me during my entire California childhood! The opportunity to grow up differently, to change the course of my life, to possibly experience a completely different environment had been, literally, just within my reach. Knowing my biological father had been just around the corner, living his life, made it even worse for me. If he had had some excuse—like being deceased, or living across the country, or living outside of the country—those reasons for being absent I could digest and comprehend. But this! This has never settled well with me, even after years of therapy and self-work.

I spent my entire childhood convinced I wasn't worthy of my biological father's love. It has been difficult to back that up into a more logical explanation after I found out that he chose not to be a part of my life. I also assumed that maybe my crazy stepdad ran him off, but my mom confirmed that they told him he needed to be in our lives, and they encouraged visitation with us. That's a tough pill to swallow. Luckily, I have done a lot of self-work in this area and, for the most part, I understand that this is my dad's issue and not mine.

Logically, I understand that I am lovable and that I deserved to have my father around when I was a child. I'm not going to lie and say that his absence still doesn't sting though—a lot. I've heard it said that, "There are only eighteen inches from your head to your heart." That's not a long distance, but most of us spend our entire lives trying to make a genuine connection between what our heads tell us and what our hearts feel. Sometimes, that eighteen inches can seem like an insurmountable distance.

My Mother

After my parents divorced, my mom met my stepdad at a bar. Like most abusers, he came across as charming and wonderful. He hid his "crazy" the first few months of their relationship. It's easy to not let it poke out and need to tuck that shit in for a short period. Norman pretended to treat my brother and I well. He convinced my mom he would be a great caretaker and provider. She told me she married him for stability, because she was a single mom with two children.

I get that. My third marriage was for the exact same reason. I didn't think I could do it on my own with two kids, so I married someone who was willing to take on all that baggage. I'm sure my mom felt the very same way when she married Norman in 1975, after dating him for only two short months. It still amazes me that, in sixty days or less, my mom decided to spend the rest of her life with this man. That's ballsy! I wonder if she had waited just a little bit longer to say, "I do," if things would have been different. Would she still have married him if she had caught just a glimpse of who he really was hidden behind that "nice guy" mask he wore? I would like to think she would not have intentionally put herself and her kids in that kind of hellish situation.

Mom's first inkling that something wasn't right came after they had already married. She was late coming home after a baby shower. It may have been her baby shower, seeing as she was already pregnant with my little brother. Mom said she arrived home about an hour later than expected, and that was when she experienced what became the first of Norman's many outbursts of rage and mental abuse. One of the things he said to her that day was that she ought to have an abortion because she was "a horrible mom."

I wish I could say I couldn't imagine being married to someone who spoke that way and said such atrocious things to me, but I do know what that's like. I have experienced this type of abuse over and over and over. I can at least sympathize with my mom, as I know what it's like to be on the receiving end of that anger. I know how it can make you feel so isolated and ashamed. Over time, you accept it, and if the abuse spans over years, you start to believe you deserve it. Even divorced from one of my abusers, I still had to endure years of text messages that went into detail as to why I was a bad mom and why, according to him, my kids hated me. Even though deep down you know it's not true, those accusations still hurt, and they still make you question yourself—especially if you're already tattered and aren't quite strong enough to let them bounce off you without effect.

In preparing to write this book, I asked my mom why she never reached out for help. I wasn't judging her. After all, I too had rarely sought assistance with my abusers. I know what my reasons were: shame, low self-worth, and fear. I was curious about what had stopped her, about why she had endured this relationship for as long as she did. Mom said she was stubborn, and in the beginning, she thought she could "fix it." I think from there it just gets very complicated. The longer you stay in an abusive relationship, the harder it is to leave. I know this to be true as I have lived it. I can speak from years of experience of trying to Houdini my way out of bad relationships.

I asked Mom if my grandmother knew what was going on. She explained that my grandma did figure things out after a while. She urged Mom to end the marriage but, for whatever reasons, my mother hung on for over twelve years. I'm also certain that Mom hid a lot of what was going on from her mother, because my grandma is not the type of person to sit idly by and let anyone terrorize her daughter or her grandkids. It's an assumption on my part, but Mom probably hid the truth about our environment out of guilt, humiliation, and maybe just a dash of fear. Also, I know my grandparents well enough to know that they would not be happy about my mom making the decision to marry someone after dating them for only two months. Maybe Mom just did not want to hear, "I told you so."

Once, before we left California, Mom did reach out for help. She reached out to the one person in her life who should have provided her with support. My mom confided in our church pastor about some of the difficulties she was having and some of the behaviors Norman was exhibiting.

I hated Sunday's more than any other day of the week. Norman forced us all to go to church and pretend we were this perfect American family. It was a charade, an act that we were forced to play out every time the church doors were open, but especially on Sundays, as that was the more formal day of worship. On Sunday's, we were forced to put on our dress clothes, smile, and pretend like everything was fine.

Everyone at the church thought our monster was a wonderful man, a model husband, and loving father. Norman, like others, used this setting to outwardly portray something he wanted the community to believe. It was sickening. It made me angry, and I have to think it made my mom angry as well. How could it not? How could it not just enrage her week after week? After church, we would come home, and the chaos would start again. The pretending would stop once Norman was in his safe place. He could behave however he wanted to behind closed doors. Someone or something or maybe nothing at all, would set him off, and once again, all hell would break loose. Holes in the wall, broken toys, lots of crying and yelling, cowering and hiding. This was our life; this was his pattern, and we knew the drill all too well.

So yes, at one point my mom found the courage to reach out to our pastor and ask him for help. In that one moment, she trusted another human being with her most humiliating secret. His response?

"If you were a better wife to Norman, he would not act the way he does."

True story.

I have been so jaded by my experiences with church that I have not stepped back into one since I left home at seventeen years of age, and I doubt I ever will again.

My mom does not like to speak about the hardships of the past. When I was forty-nine, and finally began talking with her about the events in this book, it was nearly impossible to drag her back into those painful memories. It's surprising and sad that it took my mom and I this long to be able to sit down and have an authentic conversation about our journey together. I could not have had these conversations if I had not done the work on myself to heal, to not be so angry anymore, to forgive, and to take ownership of my part and my poor decision making. It does make me sad that we could not communicate like this throughout our lives, but I understand now that I had to provide a safe place for my mom, a blame-free space, for her to be able to speak freely about such emotional topics. In the same way that speaking my truth in these pages is helping me overcome the shame and embarrassment of my story and enabling me to take back the power that was stolen from me for so long, I hope that having these honest discussions with my mom, where she too can speak her truth, will help her experience closure, healing, and greater inner peace.

PART TWO

MY TEEN YEARS

FIVE

The Move

"Stand up for yourself and your rights as a human being.
You are strong. You are beautiful.
And there is more to life than walking on eggshells."
Domestic Violence Survivor

I was born in Oakland, California and raised in the Bay Area. Growing up as a latchkey kid, I had a lot of freedom. Because both my mom and stepdad worked, I was at liberty to roam the city until the streetlights came on. That was my signal that it was time to go home. The weekends were the same. I would sometimes leave in the morning and be gone all day, traveling as far as my bike or roller skates would take me.

I loved the independence and freedom I had growing up. My friends and I were fearless. We'd take public transportation, sometimes deep into the city, to go see a movie or just explore. That part of my childhood I would not trade for anything. That part of my childhood gave me useful bricks to add to my foundation, bricks of independence and self-reliance.

That's why I was so very, very angry, in 1984, to learn that, instead of starting high school in the Bay Area, I was to begin high school in a totally different part of the country. The year I turned thirteen I was told we were moving to Arkansas—a state that my friends and I hadn't heard of and that we certainly couldn't spell! I was angry about leaving a city that allowed me so much freedom and independence. I was angry at the idea of leaving my friends and the schools I grew up with. Even though my beloved grandparents had moved there several years earlier, I still didn't want to go.

I look back on this now and realize that fear was at the root of my anger. Fear was the emotion I was really feeling; the anger was just how I chose to deal with it, to process it. I was afraid of my life being turned upside down and of losing what little stability I had. I feared losing my friends and having to make new ones. I was also afraid of being so far away from my biological father as I still hoped that someday I might be able to be part of his life. I feared standing out and being different. But most of all, I feared the unknown.

I was so scared and angry about moving that I voiced my displeasure to my mom many, many times. To try and combat my arguing, she arranged for me to spend the summer before high school with my grandparents in Arkansas. Mom figured it was a way to ease me into the transition, give me time to acclimate to the area, and maybe even make some friends before school started.

To say that I went through extreme culture shock when I arrived in Arkansas is an understatement. It felt like I had literally been transported to another planet!

From the beginning, my siblings and I stood out like a sore thumb. The first day of high school, my older brother and I rolled up to the school with me looking like Madonna and him looking like the character of Crockett from *Miami Vice*. I was sent home to change since apparently, Arkansas school administrators frown upon black lace attire that displays one's belly button! Back home in California, I blended in with every other teenage girl. In this new world, I certainly did not blend—not just because of fashion, but also because I had fully adopted the Valley girl language. I spoke insanely fast. I don't think the kids understood me half the time, and I was frustrated by their slow, southern drawl and thick accent. To me, it was painful to have a conversation because it seemed to take people forever to get a sentence out. With time, the Valley girl was overtaken by the southern girl, and now, you would never even guess that I came from the Bay Area.

Best Summer of My Childhood

Despite the culture shock and my fears, anger, and vehement arguments against the move, that Arkansas summer—the one before I started high school—ended up being the best summer of my childhood. Staying with my grandparents, I was free from my stepdad and the nightmare that had been my environment. For the first time since I was four years old, I was free from the daily burden of having to walk on eggshells so as to not upset Norman. My grandparents loved me, and cared for me, and I didn't even mind that they could be a bit strict. Their home on a dirt road in a small town felt like a safe place for me. I managed to make a few friends that lived close by, and we spent the entire summer hanging out.

I did things I never could have done in the Bay Area. I learned how to ride a horse. I hauled hay with my friends for extra cash. I rode a mini-bike and swam in creeks. I also got to have fun with two cousins who were close to my age, since soon after my grandparents moved, my aunt and uncle had moved right next door to them.

That summer I was able to experience what "normal" looked like. I was able to wake up without stress and go to bed listening to the sounds of frogs instead of the sound of my monster screaming at someone. That summer was the first time I truly felt like the person I was meant to be. I was happy. I was not a thug. I was not the Valley girl who had begun to fight, drink and smoke. Those were just more coping mechanisms I developed to hide the pain that was consuming me. When I was with my grandparents, I was at peace. And because I was content, I did not fight, I did not drink, and I did not get into any trouble. I did not act out at all. I was merely a kid enjoying the summer, reveling in new experiences.

My Second Brush with Death

There was only one day that summer when I disobeyed my grandmother. Looking back, I believe we are all glad I did.

On that particular day, I was hanging out at my friends' house when my grandpa came by in his pickup truck. He said he needed to make a trip to town and, since my grandma was not up for it, she had instructed him to take me along. For some reason, Grandma never liked Grandpa to go anywhere alone. Being thirteen years old, I was at that age where I would rather hang with my friends than be tasked with this burden. I selfishly begged Grandpa to let me stay, to not force me to go into town with him. Reluctantly, he agreed, yelling, "Don't tell your grandma!" out the window as he drove off.

I can't remember if he ever made it to town to do his errands or if the wreck occurred on the way home. A young adult hit my grandfather head on, and the impact resulted in Grandpa breaking his neck. He survived, which at his age was incredible in itself, but he certainly did not come out of it unscathed. The doctors had to use one of those halo apparatus things that screwed into his head to stabilize his neck. The rest of the summer was not only difficult for my grandfather, it was also very hard on me and my grandma as we spent most of our time taking care of him.

There's a part of me that has always felt incredibly guilty for disobeying Grandma, because maybe if I had been with Grandpa, he would have never gotten into that car accident. On the other hand, if I had obeyed Grandma, and the accident occurred just as it did, I would have been crushed by the engine. That's the part of this story that still makes me shudder to this day. The impact of the crash pushed the truck's motor into the passenger's seat, into the exact spot where I would have been sitting.

Grandma never asked me why I had not gone to town with Grandpa. I think she knew what would have happened if I had done as she wished. I think she was relieved that I defied her—just this once—and cheated death for the second time.

When I was forty-nine and questioning my mom about our move to Arkansas, she told me the main reason she made that decision was because she wanted a divorce. She was strategically trying to position herself both financially, and in proximity to her parents and my aunt and uncle, to have the support that would enable her to get out of the marriage. Her plan worked, eventually, but it took my mother four more years to leave Norman after the initial move. I get how that happened, because I have been in a similar position on several occasions. These experiences taught me that sometimes, having support around you and the financial means makes or breaks your ability to get away from your abuser.

SIX

The House from Hell

"Rebellion is a sign of a child fighting
to be seen as who they are."
Carol Tuttle

My brief taste of something normal, of what it was like to live in a house where you did not have to be on edge all the time, came to a screeching halt at the end of the summer I stayed with my grandparents. It felt almost cruel to be allowed to sample a loving environment, only to have it ripped away and be forced to go back to the hell that was life with Norman. But that's what happened, just at the start of my high school years, when our house in California sold and the rest of my family moved to Arkansas. I was pulled from my grandparents' protection and thrust into a situation that was even worse than what I left in California.

There were three reasons for the downward spiral that was to be my life for the next four years. The first was the fact that my entering puberty was met with new abuses, which I have shared previously. The second reason for the downward spiral was the rebellious behaviors I began to engage in when I entered my teen years. My rebellion made our family dynamics even more difficult for everyone. It made it harder for my mom, day in and day out. The only way she could try and protect me, or my brother, was to hide as much as she could from the monster. I knew she was covering for me and that probably made me act out more. This went beyond normal teenager rebellion because I was very, very angry during this period of my life.

The third reason for the worsening of my situation had to do with the house that my mom and stepfather bought when they first moved to Arkansas. I "lovingly" refer to it as the "house from hell." Of all the options they had, they moved to a very small town, and within that small town, they chose to get a house with one bedroom. That's right; just one bedroom with three kids. I was told, "We plan on building on to the house so that everyone will have their own rooms." That never happened. No attempt was made to better our living situation, and the years we lived there were the worst I can remember from my childhood.

My mom and stepdad slept in the living room on a pull-out sofa. My older brother slept in the garage using boxes as walls. At first, my little brother and I slept in bunk beds in the one bedroom. I was a teenage girl and desperately needed some space and privacy. The only option for me was to put a bed on the screened in porch. It wasn't very private, but it was an improvement from a bunk bed. So that's what I did. The winters could get very cold, so I had a heater for that season and a fan for the summer months. There was a door on the porch that led to a small cellar. It always creeped me out at night. For many reasons, I was never completely comfortable in that space. Maybe it was because it seemed more like a homeless shelter than a home.

Our living conditions were not ideal even for a healthy family unit. These quarters just magnified the chaos and dysfunction of our already toxic environment and subjected everyone to added stress. I was rarely home because I spent most of my time at my best friend's house. My brother, who is two years older than me, was also gone most of time. He worked and played football. Like my older stepbrothers from Nevada, my brother had also grown to be a large young man, too big for my stepfather to torment. Needing a new victim, Norman turned his focus on me. But the older I got, the less scared I was of my childhood monster. I stood up to him more and more; I pushed back more and more. One of the times I pushed back resulted in me being chased out of the house by my knife-wielding stepfather as he threatened to kill me.

That day, Norman struck my mom in front of me as the two of them argued. Something inside of me snapped and I lost my mind. I was tired of the abuse, I was tired of the yelling, I was tired of Norman. I began screaming at him and was unafraid for the first time that I can remember. I ran at him yelling, "If you touch her again, I will fucking kill you!" The rage and adrenaline rushed through my veins like I had just taken a hit of cocaine. The power I felt in that moment was intoxicating. I had no plan, I had no weapon to defend myself, and yet I felt like I was ten feet tall—invincible!

Norman was not accustomed to seeing that lack of fear in my eyes and I don't think he liked it. The only way he knew how to respond was to escalate to more violence, more fear. Grabbing a kitchen knife out of the butcher's block, he turned on me, scream-ing, "I'm going to kill you, you fucking bitch!"

My mom and I ran outside where she called my older brother for assistance; not the cops to protect me and her, but my older brother. When he pulled up in the driveway, we were still huddled outside. That's when he and the monster got into a physical con-frontation.

Why didn't we flee? Why didn't we seek protective shelter? At the time, I could not make sense of my mother's decisions. I never understood why she didn't call the police on my stepdad that day, or any other day for that matter. I never understood it until I was in the exact same position, faced with the same decisions, and I too never called the police on any of my abusers. For too many years, I also chose not to flee, or seek safety and shelter. I made those choices partly due to fear, partly due to ego, and partly due to not feeling like I deserved a better life.

Sneaking Out

There was one benefit to living in the house from hell: sleeping on the back porch made it easier to sneak out at night. Directly be-hind us was an orchard. I simply had to go out the screen door and run through the orchard to freedom. This was a frequent activity, and I never once got caught—not even when I got picked up by the local police.

That night, my best friend and I snuck out of my house to meet some boys. After meeting at a previously agreed upon spot, we drove to a creek together and started drinking. I don't think the guys had nearly the amount of alcohol that my friend and I con-sumed. They watched in amusement as us two girls decided that playing in the creek would be a good idea. It was all innocent fun really, but we got nailed because my friend and I made too much noise, screeching with delight as the cold water soaked us. Someone from a nearby house yelled, "We're calling the cops!"

"Hmm," we wondered. "What's the wisest thing to do in this situation?" Try to outrun the police, of course! We piled in the car and tore down the dirt road like a bunch of hooligans. At one point, we thought it would be clever to pull into a random driveway and shut the car off in the hope that the police would not be able to spot us. It sounded like a good plan . . . but it wasn't. The cops pulled in right behind us, with lights flashing.

The policemen called the boys' parents, who came and picked them up. Then the officers had me and my girlfriend to contend with. I told the sob story that if they called my parents, my stepdad would beat the ever-living shit out of me. I begged them to allow me to sneak back into my house so as to avoid such abuse. My friend was spending the night with me, so it would allow both of us to escape the consequences of our little adventure. Can you believe they agreed to it? Thank God for small town America!

So here we were, riding in the back of a cop car, very drunk, very hungry, and completely oblivious to how much trouble we could be in, not just from the police, but from Norman. I found the cop's lunch, or breakfast rather, in the back seat and decided it looked too good to pass up. My friend and I ate that poor man's food! We made a lot of bad decisions that night but somehow managed to come out of it intact. There was also some singing to the radio and most certainly some giggling on the way home. The police officer had to have been relieved to dump us off at the corner of my house and the orchard. We successfully snuck back into

my room that was the screened in porch and no one was ever the
wiser.

SEVEN

My First Job

"One man's transparency is another's humiliation."

Gerry Adams

There are so many stories related to my stepdad that I had to determine which ones to share to paint the clearest picture of why I came out of my childhood so broken and lost, so vulnerable to letting others treat me as less than human later in life. The story of how I got my first job is one of those accounts.

By my senior year in high school, we had finally moved out of the wretched "house from hell" and to another city a little further north. This put us outside the school district I had been in. Since I was not about to change schools my senior year, I drove back and forth to my old school every day.

I had been looking for a job and putting in applications. Back then, you had to go and physically fill out applications. I was looking forward to working because it meant independence and being away from the four walls that imprisoned me. But even though I looked forward to the escape a job would provide, I found it difficult to concentrate when searching for one, and I had no guidance from any adult as to how to go about the process.

One day I found myself alone in the house with my monster. We were sitting at the dining room table and he was screaming at me about the fact that I did not yet have a job. I was crying as he towered over me, wild-eyed, yelling at the loudest possible decibel. Even at sixteen years old (I was a young senior), Norman could still make me feel like a defenseless child. As he screamed and degraded me, I did what I had done so often in my teenage years to distract myself during his angry sessions. I shut out the noise, blurred his face as best I could by squinting slightly and looking over him but not directly at him. Then I imagined myself just hauling off and punching him square in the face. How good would it feel to actually do that? Would it be worth the consequences? I think it might have been, but I was never brave enough to try it.

Just down the road was a strip mall that had a movie theater and a fast-food restaurant. Norman made me get in the car and we sped off to that strip mall. He was so upset with me that he literally dragged me inside its fast-food place by my hair. He was still screaming at me, but this time we were in a public setting. I was so humiliated that I started crying again. I tried so hard not to cry and was disappointed in myself that I could not hold back the tears. I did not want everyone around me to witness my shame, to see that I was weak and helpless. At the age of sixteen, I wanted to believe I had some power, even if just a little, but it was painfully clear that I did not.

Letting go of my hair, Norma grabbed my arm, dragged me

to the counter, and demanded an application from the startled teenager working there. We sat in a booth where I filled out the application and tried to pretend that nothing abnormal was occurring. "Nothing to see here," I thought to myself. I wished it was a different scenario where I had a sympathetic parent with me to oversee the process because I was nervous and unsure about how to find a job. I wished I was receiving love, and support, and nurturing guidance through this adulting rite of passage. I wished it was something other than the ugly truth. I sat silently, and the tears fell, as I attempted to fill out the work application.

I briefly began to drift into an old coping mechanism, drawn back to those fantasies I used to visualize as a kid, different scenarios that would take my monster away from us; death, divorce, or just plain disappearing. Then the smell of grease and french fries jolted me back to my current reality; the reality that I was sitting in a fast-food restaurant with my monster, visible, for all the world to see. It was one of the only times I can ever remember where Norman failed to put his mask on in public. That was the day I realized I preferred the mask. I preferred to suffer quietly. I preferred for the whole world to not know about my secret existence.

A strained silence fell over the establishment as everyone pretended not to watch this cluster fuck, but it was like a bad car wreck. You don't want to see it, but somehow you can't help but stare. The employees did their best to pretend they were busy, but it was obvious they were distracted by us, and probably feeling bad and embarrassed for me. The customers pretended to ignore what was going on and minded their own business. Part of me was angry that everyone just politely looked away. Part of me wanted someone to stand up to my six-foot-seven monster and be an advocate for me. I needed someone to be my voice as I was unable to find my own. I was looking for my Prince Charming to come rescue me, but he never showed up.

I somehow managed to complete and turn in the application, although I could not even make eye contact with the young kid at the counter. I was too humiliated. It was a blessing that we were in a different town than where I was attending high school. I did not know any of these kids, so the gossip about this tragic scene would not spread like wildfire through my school. I had managed to keep the truth about my home life a secret from even my best friends, and I did not want that secret to be exposed at this point.

Ironically, I ended up getting an interview, which I have no doubt was just a pity interview. Regardless, I did get a job at that restaurant and worked there for about a year, before changing jobs. It was one of my favorite places to work as the job itself was not difficult, and I enjoyed being around my co-workers. In the end, my monster's parenting technique was certainly effective. Norman got the outcome he desired; I became employed.

Unfortunately for me, the messages of unworthiness and humiliation that my brain received that day continued to feed what I now compassionately call my "Dark Side." This term was taught to me later, as I went through therapy, to name the shame and the heaviness that sat on my shoulder every day. I did not know back then that the voices in my head, that filled my thoughts with fallacies and negative energy, were this Dark Side that started to run my life. I did not realize, until later in my adult life, that my

Dark Side was the sum of all the harmful messaging I had received from all my abusers. These derogatory voices were permanently perched on my shoulder in the form of an invisible, heavy darkness, that were always whispering, "I told you that you are not enough." The fallout from this day fed my darkness and gave me a couple more bricks; more broken bricks that added to the foundation of lies about my self-worth upon which I was forced to build my young life.

EIGHT

My First Love

*"Don't allow yourself to think that toxic love
is the best love that you can ever have."*

Author unknown

Johnny was my high school boyfriend and my first love. I'm not sure exactly what attracted me to him. It may have been that everything about Johnny was a red flag—from the cigarettes he smoked to the red motorcycle he roared around on—and I liked the idea of being with someone who was just as much of a hot mess as I was. Or it may have been his insanely good looks. With his long, wavy dark hair and a full-blown, Tom Selleck mustache, Johnny looked much older than the other teenage boys. Chances are it was a mixture of all these things.

Johnny was new to our school during our sophomore year. All the girls immediately began clawing each other for his attention. He looked like he just stepped out of the movie *The Outsiders*, and back then, that was pure sex appeal for us teenage girls.

Johnny did not start with me. He made his rounds with some of the girls, eventually stopping at me. We dated for almost two years, although honestly, I'm not very confident he wasn't messing around during some, or all, of that period.

Norman hated Johnny from the very beginning, so much so that once he even punched Johnny, full-on, Mike Tyson to the face. On that particular day, Johnny had come over to the house to pick me up, and the two men began to argue about whether or not we were having sex. Johnny was smug and unafraid of Norman, and I think that made my stepfather angrier. Norman reacted in the only way he knew how—violence. He punched Johnny square in the jaw.

My *loving* stepdad, who I'm *sure* was just worried about my wellbeing, had found my diary and read it. The entire thing. That's when he found out Johnny and I were sexually active, and that was how he chose to deal with the situation. Norman woke up every day and chose violence. That was always the "go to" choice for him.

After my monster chased off the man whom I, at that time, saw as the love of my life, he then proceeded to tell me I could never see Johnny again. Challenge accepted! Knowing that Johnny elicited such a visceral reaction from my monster only made me want to be with him more. In typical teenage fashion, I defiantly continued to see Johnny, but hid those interactions from Norman. I know my mom knew about us, and she hid it from Norman too, just like she concealed everything else.

My stepdad eventually gave up trying to restrict access when he realized I never stopped seeing Johnny. We drove right by Norman one day and oh . . . the look on his face as the cars passed each other! It was a look of pure outrage! I stayed away from the house for as long as possible before I finally went home to face the music. That was the only time I ever remember Norman just giving up. There were no temper tantrums, name calling, or other punishments I had to endure. Maybe he was just tired, maybe he was just getting more mellow in his old age, or maybe I just caught him on one of his "highs." Whatever the reason, he stopped fighting Johnny's and my relationship. Words cannot express the strength I felt inside of me when I realized I had won a battle against Norman.

Meanwhile, I was completely consumed with Johnny and our relationship. I found comfort in the fact that I was with someone who also had a shitty homelife. Johnny's parents were divorced, and his mother was never around to monitor his activities or his younger brother's, which left Johnny to take care of him. His mom rarely come home at night, and even though we primarily hung out at his house, I only saw her one time in almost two years. I'm almost certain his mom was an alcoholic, which made his life chaotic and unhinged. Their house was always trashed, and not just cluttered, but a level of disgusting I had not seen before. Given the dysfunctionality of both our families, we understood each other. We didn't have to pretend around each other.

I had my sights on marrying Johnny when we graduated, but he had other plans. The last part of our senior year, Johnny finally got fed up with his mom and left the state to go live with his dad. Before he left, our relationship had pretty much run its course; we were about done anyway. I was desperately trying to hang on to what was left, but he had checked out months ago. He wasn't abusive or mean in any way, but he was distracted. I caught him, at least once, cheating on me near the end of our relationship.

This occurrence was one of the many crossroads I arrived at during my life. What I should have done was dump his sorry ass, because I deserved better than that. The thing was, I did not believe that I deserved better. In fact, what I felt was gratitude that someone like Johnny chose to be with me at all. This backwards thinking set the stage for me as I forgave him and allowed the indiscretion. This inability to demand better for myself continued throughout much of my adult life.

My solution to the problem of Johnny cheating on me was to track down his other woman in a mall parking lot where I tried to beat the shit out of her. My solution to this problem was violence. This is not who I was; that behavior was taught to me by my monster.

When Johnny left the state and me, I really began to fall apart. I attempted to replace the pain of my loss with alcohol, drinking to fill the void and to forget how sad I was. I even drank at school a few times, putting vodka in a water bottle and sipping on it throughout the day. I'm not even sure why I did this because it never helped. I never liked feeling numb and out of control. I just didn't know how to deal with the overwhelming pain I was experiencing. Johnny was a distraction from my life, and now I no longer had that distraction. I felt like I was only visible when he was around. It was the first time in my life I had felt truly loved by someone, even if that love was not perfect, or maybe not even real. When Johnny left, I just wanted to finish dying because I already felt dead inside.

The pain of my loss was so intense that I remember sitting outside on our deck crying one night. My mom came out to check on me, which means I must have been out there for a while for her to come looking for me. I told her I wanted to kill myself. I didn't really mean it, as I was too chicken shit to do something like that, but I could not find the words to express just how badly I was hurting. That is what came out of my mouth. I don't think she quite knew how to handle the situation, so she just told me, "Quit talking crazy, and get inside the house."

There were only two times in my life I contemplated suicide, and that was one of them. Luckily, this first instance was just a mere thought and nothing more. The second time would be a bit more serious.

Just a few months after Johnny left the state, I received a letter in the mail with a picture of him snuggled up to some chick. This mystery girl wrote the letter. She told me they were in love, they were getting married, and not to contact him anymore. We did not have cell phones back then, so all I had left of Johnny was the address he scribbled down on a piece of paper. I was still clinging to the hope that after I graduated, I would move to where he was living, and we would get back together. I wanted him and I to get married, not him and some mystery chick.

I wrote a couple letters to Johnny, but that letter and picture were the only response I ever received. Johnny never once wrote back to me himself, which showed me how little he thought of me. The only way I knew how to deal with this crushing new pain was to hide behind lots of partying. I would surround myself with all my friends and drown myself in alcohol. That would continue to be my coping mechanism well into my twenties.

NINE

My High School Career

*"Don't be upset by the results you didn't get
with the work you didn't do."*

Author unknown

High school in Arkansas wasn't so bad. For the most part, I welcomed the distraction of classes and extracurricular activities and I enjoyed being with my friends. It was a small school, so everyone knew everyone. There were less than a hundred people in my graduation class of 1989. I liked the fact that there were not any real clicks and that I had friends in every group imaginable. I don't remember any bullying or "mean girl" behavior like I saw at the bigger schools in California. Those schools had so many kids you could go to the same school system all twelve years and still not know everyone. Sometimes, I liked that scenario better because it made it easier to be invisible; to fade into the background. Since I could not do that in Arkansas, I decided to put myself out front as the class clown and troublemaker. I adopted this façade while, at the same time, hiding the horrors of my home life and concealing the girl behind the mask.

To my friends, I was the life of the party. If something mischievous was going on, I was usually right in the middle of it, or I was the ringleader. I skipped a lot of school. If Johnny wasn't there, I would cut class and go hang out with him at his place. On other days, my best friend and I would skip and go hang out at this small lake that was not too far from our homes. We never did anything bad or harmful; we just didn't feel like being in class on nice days.

In fact, I missed so much school that I barely graduated. My grades were fine; I just had technically missed more days than I was supposed to for graduation privileges. The principal actually called my mom and told her they were going to graduate me anyways because, "We love her, but we just don't want her back." That was a nice way to say, "We've had enough of her shit."

Disappearing to be Visible

I tried to run away twice during my high school years. The first time, my best friend was the one who thought of the idea and even picked tour destination. She was either upset over a boy, or upset with her parents, or both. Her reasons didn't matter to me because I was always up for anything; any chance to escape was a good idea in my book. Any opportunity to get attention—even negative attention—to be seen, to feel like I mattered, was always inviting to me. Johnny and I were on and off again at that point, so a small part of me hoped this would get his attention. Sadly, it did not. I don't think it even fazed him that I was gone for three whole days.

When I told my best friend I would gladly accompany her on this grand adventure she bought us two Greyhound bus tickets to her grandmother's town in Colorado. We arrived at Grandma's house without incident, but it didn't take Grandma long to call my friend's parents. My friend's mom immediately called my mom who told me that my stepdad was so pissed that he did not want me in the house. That made me smile. When she told me I had to come home but I had to go stay with my grandparents, that made me smile even more. I never actually thought about what my consequences would be for running away, but this was actually the best outcome I could have. We only got to stay in Colorado a couple of days before we had to board a plane and fly home. I didn't stay with my grandparents for long, but still . . . it was a nice break.

The second time I ran away from home was during my junior year in high school. Technically, it was more like a planned escape than a true attempt to run away, seeing as my mom knew and consented to my destination. In this instance, I thought I was running towards stability and a better environment, but I ran smack into something that was even more chaotic than what I left behind. I could not catch a break!

Prior to this escape, my mom had separated from Norman. During those blissful days, my mom, my younger brother, and I lived in a little duplex just down the road from school. My older brother had already graduated high school and moved into an apartment of his own. With Norman gone, I was so happy that I never caused any trouble. I went to school, I did not sneak out, and I behaved myself. I thought if I made things easier on my mom, she would be okay on her own.

One night I came home and found Norman in bed with my mother. I immediately felt sick to my stomach. I wanted to puke because I knew what this meant. The monster was back. That is why I left home the second time. My mom broke the news to us that she was moving back in with Norman and I could not bear it. I told her, "No way in hell am I ever living with that man again!"

My mom allowed me to go live with my brother in his apartment. My brother was in extreme party mode when I moved in. He partied and drank most nights. His friends and girlfriend were over constantly. Although he was only two years older than me, they were all out of high school, but I was not. They lived off pizza and beer and, for a short time, it seemed like a teenager's dream . . . until it wasn't.

The car I had been driving was not running at the time. Since I had no wheels, I was completely reliant on my brother to transport me back and forth from school. This quickly become problematic when he was too hung over in the morning to take me to class. I missed even more school during this short stint with him. Without transportation, it was difficult to get to work or to try and find something other than pizza to eat. The late nights and the chaos started to become too much for me. Deep down inside, what I really craved was structure and a calm environment. My brother's apartment was neither of those things.

As I reflected on my situation, I realized that when living with my mother and Norman, I did not have to worry about food and transportation and I had my own room. It wasn't long before I went crawling back to monster. That was the hardest part for me, having to ask to come back home.

Prom

I went to my junior prom while living with my brother. Johnny backed out on going with me at the last minute, saying he had to work. He didn't have to work. He was just done with me and didn't want to go. At that point we were mostly "off," but I was still hanging on, hoping things would get better.

My brother and one of his friends had offered to escort me to the dance, but the last thing I wanted was to show up at prom with my older brother or with a pity date. I was trying to hang on to what little dignity I had from being brushed off by Johnny. I wasn't thrilled about going without a date, and I almost backed out of the whole thing. But I had some other friends going stag, so I chose to tag along with them. After all, teenage girls live for these events. We want to get dressed up in fairytale dresses, and hope that the night will be magical. My night was far from fairytale or magical.

My mom came over to help me get ready because she wanted to be part of the event. I feel guilty now for the way I treated her that night, but back then, my anger at her going back to monster and choosing him over us was an open wound that had not healed.

Getting ready at my brothers and not at home made me feel more empowered, like somehow, I finally had some sort of control over the situation. Power and control were what I had always longed for as a child, but never had. That false sense of power ignited my fury, and I lashed out at my mother. We argued over my attitude towards her, and at the height of the arguing, I called her "a selfish bitch." That was the one and only time she ever slapped me.

The rest of my night pretty much went downhill from there. How could I possibly enjoy prom without a date, with the sting of my mother's slap still smarting on my cheek, and with guilt starting to weigh on me? I wore the night like a heavy blanket, and that's where my memory ends. I don't recall what happened during or after prom; there's just a vague recollection of an after-party somewhere. I most likely dragged myself back to my brother's apartment sometime early the next morning, hungover and full of regret.

The night my mom came over to help me get ready for prom she took some photos of me. We found one of them the day I went over to interview her for this book. I studied that photograph and was saddened when I looked into my teenage eyes. The hurt was so apparent. Memories of that day came rushing back to me. There was a brief moment, as my mom and I argued, when I thought, "I don't want you here." But the truth is, I did want her there. Throughout my childhood and high school years, I always wanted my mom with me, in every aspect of my life. I just wanted her there without Norman. The irony is, she was always there, but I was never in a place to realize it, and more importantly, to appreciate it.

My entire high school career, I masked my internal pain with goofing off and humor. Making people laugh made me popular. I made Homecoming and Color's Day court a couple years. I was on the Drill Team for a couple years. My senior year I was voted Class Clown, Best Sense of Humor, and Biggest Break Up. (I could have done without this last one—thank you very much, Johnny). I was smart and made good grades, when I applied myself. A few teachers saw my potential and pushed me to succeed. Unfortunately, I let those teachers down, and I let myself down because I never truly engaged in school. I could have gone on to college and accomplished great things with my life. Sadly, I did not apply myself often, so I did not go on to higher education at that point. After I graduated from high school, it would be almost another thirty years before I obtained my college degree.

TEN

Escaping

"I guess no matter how hard you try,
you can't escape your past."
Joel Osteen

By my senior year of high school, I was fortunate enough to have two best friends, Louise, whom I joined in her attempt to run away, and Barbara, who was the nicest, most caring soul I had ever met. That's why I wanted to be around Barbara—hell, I even wanted to *be* Barbara—because she had a comforting warmth to her that was soothing. Because of this, Barbara was very popular at school. She was a bit shy, but kind to everyone.

Husband #1 - Peter

During senior year, I met my first husband, Peter, through Barbara. Okay . . . so that's kind of true, but there's a little more to the story. Barbara was dating Peter at the time, but her heart was not in the relationship. She actually had a huge crush on another boy at school. I was not particularly attracted to Peter physically, but I was very attracted to the way he treated Barbara, to the acts of kindness he showed her. That's why, when I found out Barbara had another love interest, I jumped at the chance to experience the warmth and love I thought Peter could provide.

When Barbara told me she wanted to break up with Peter, but she did not want to hurt his feelings, I came up with an ingenious plan designed to ease the pain they would both experience—which would also serve *my* purpose. I told Barbara I would ask Peter out after she dumped him. Believe it or not, that crazy plan actually worked! In fact, it worked so well that Barbara married the guy she had a crush on—they are still together to this day–and I married Peter! He and I dated the latter part of my senior year, went to senior prom together, moved in with each other when I was seventeen years old, and married when I was only eighteen.

Up to that point, with the exception of my grandfather, the men in my life had done nothing but erode my self-esteem and give me broken bricks upon which to build the foundation of my young life. Abandoned by my biological father and abused by my stepfather, I thought I had found love with my boyfriend, Johnny. But the way he just up and left me, moving to another state and hooking up with some girl he married within just a few months, made me feel like I'd never really mattered to him. Based on these experiences, it never dawned on me that maybe the world was filled with wonderful guys. That's why, when Peter came along, I thought I needed to grab him if I ever wanted to have someone who would be kind to me.

I also saw marriage as a way out of the house and away from my stepfather. If I had stopped, just for a moment, and thought it through, I would have realized I had other options that would have provided an escape. I had other routes now that I was graduating high school and would soon be an adult. I could have obtained student loans and went away to college, but with my low academic achievement and history of skipping school, no one ever provided any guidance regarding furthering my education. Besides, college was never my focus. Surviving was my focus. Getting out of the house and finding something different was my focus.

Having not done any work on myself this early in my life, I did not understand that my behavior was self-destructive, and I certainly didn't know how to stop it. The ironic thing is that my mother finally gathered up the courage to divorce Norman for good in 1989, the same year I graduated high school. I didn't have to run anymore, but I didn't even realize it! By this point, I was so desperate that I was not thinking clearly. I was just seventeen, and the only future I could envision was just surviving day-to-day.

So that was my decision, to marry at eighteen, and my mother did nothing to stop me. I have no doubt that, after the hell I put her through in high school, she was just glad that someone had stepped up and claimed me. Now that I was no longer under her roof, I would be someone else's problem. I have no doubt that my mother was simply exhausted.

My First Child

I regret putting my first husband in the position I did. I expected Peter to save me, fix me, heal me, and make up for the pain of heart. I thought that he alone could make everything better. He never had a chance.

To make matters worse, I was convinced that having a child together would make my life complete and our marriage strong. I also believed that having a baby would solve all my problems, and fix the lack of love I felt in my marriage, and the lack of love I had for myself.

I purposely got pregnant as soon as we married. I had morning sickness so bad that there were days I could not even get out of bed. Together, we decided it would be best if I quit my job and we tried to operate financially with me being a stay-at-home mom.

The three of us lived in a run-down mobile home that had a wood stove and no central heat and air. It was located next door to Peter's parents, on top of a mountain, and it came with free rent. The trailer was extremely isolated from town. What made things even more claustrophobic, was that we had only one, rundown vehicle, so I did not get to go anywhere most days. I was soon stuck in a daily rut of watching soap operas, doing my exercises, taking care of my son, and cooking dinner. As a way to entertain myself, I began pouring through cookbooks to find new recipes and desserts. I didn't particularly enjoy this; I was just trying to fill the time until Peter came home after work.

While I enjoyed being a mom and caring for my son, the day-to-day routine and isolation of my life was numbing. It was not long before I became miserable. I felt trapped, like a caged rabbit. I now recognize that I had become trapped by my own doing, but nevertheless, I felt trapped. I wanted a job. I wanted my freedom, I wanted to go see what was out there in the world. The grass had turned greener on the other side and I wanted to run through it and never look back.

My son was not even a year old when I made the decision to leave my first husband, even though we were great friends and he treated me well. With Peter and I, it was truly a case of, "It's not you, it's me." As an adult, I have heard the saying "Happiness is an inside job." I so wish I had understood this concept early on! Our marriage was not the issue; my broken bricks and empty heart were the problem. My low self-esteem and abandonment issues were the problem.

I was divorced for the first time by the age of twenty-one. My ex and his family talked me into sharing custody of my son. They convinced me that this arrangement would be best for all of us. I was naïve, and I could not afford a huge lawyer bill. I believed them when they said that they would help financially, and that we would co-parent, and that it would all work out beautifully. I trusted the friendship that my husband and I once had, but was unaware that his mom was now running the show.

It did not work out beautifully. I received no child support and had no help raising my son during my weeks of visitation. This decision, like many others, would come back to bite me again and again for the next few years.

PART THREE

MY ROARING TWENTIES

ELEVEN

Girls Just Wanna Have Fun

*"Numbing the pain for a while will make
it worse when you finally feel it."*
Albus Dumbledore

After my first divorce, I finally experienced the freedom I had been craving. I was only twenty-one, so it's no surprise that there was a period of a few years where I just wanted to have fun; no relationships, no responsibility, no one trying to tear me down, no one controlling me, and no marriage. I used to think poorly of myself for behaving in such a wild and loose and manner, but I've come to understand it was a necessity. I needed to get it out of my system so I could move on. For just a short time, I needed to have fun in my life, even if it was not the healthiest type of fun. I needed to make my own decisions; I needed to make my own mistakes.

I fell in with a large group of people, most of whom were ten years older than myself. The group began with just a couple of people, and grew over time. At the end of this early '90s era, we had quite a large squad that hung out regularly. We mostly hung out at this one bar where we would drink, sing karaoke, and dance. There were a few of us that attended live concerts on a regular basis.

I had a decent job that I liked well enough, but because I was not making much money, I bounced around regarding my living conditions. I lived with friends mostly, but for a short period, I had my own apartment. I liked that situation the best. They were nice apartments, and the complex had a pool and a gym. My mom even gave me some of her old furniture that had been hand-me-downs from my grandparents. I was happy there. I don't remember why I moved on from that place; probably I could not afford it long-term.

Some of my friends experimented with drugs, but that never interested me. Alcohol was my pain reliever of choice. My biggest regret is how much time I spent at the bars or at concerts, instead of spending that time with my young son. Of course, I would make sure I had a sitter when he was in my care and I was out at night. But I should have stayed home more. I should have also created a more stable environment for him by not moving around so much. I was not the mom I had hoped to be, and my destructive behavior was selfish. While I do recognize that I was doing the best I could at the time, I also know that my best was not that great. Thank God my "girls just wanna have fun" phase did not last for too many years.

Glimpsing the Depths of My Anger

I had always known I was angry about my life, about what had occurred when I was younger. I knew I was angry at my dad for abandoning me, my stepdad for his abuse, and my mom for not protecting me. What I didn't know was just how very, very angry I was and just how very, very far down I had shoved that anger.

My first glimpses into the depths of my anger occurred during my twenties. What I saw was terrifying. To know that an emotion could engulf me to the point where I had no control was deeply unsettling, especially since I am not a violent or aggressive person by nature. The only two bar fights I have ever been in are what showed me the depth of my anger.

Both fights occurred within the same year and at the same bar where my friends and I hung out all week, every week. Since we were usually there on the weekends as well, we were well known by the manager and the employees. There was a side of the bar that was for dancing, and there was a side of the bar that was more chill. You could sing karaoke on some nights and even have appetizers. This bar was my home away from home for at least two years.

The more vivid of the two fights was not a one-on-one thing. It was a full-on bar brawl, instigated by my big mouth.

It was a typical weekend night, and I was at the bar with my crew. With our large group of friends, it was not uncommon for six, eight, or sometimes more of us to be together at once. This night was no different. A few of us girls were hanging out on the dance side of the club, drinking our Long Island Ice Teas. Being regulars, we were typically given a lot of free drinks and the best seats in the house. I don't think that being a group of mostly young, scantily dressed girls hurt our favored status either.

This one evening, a group of girls showed up that we had not seen before. These girls were all heftier than us, and from the get-go, they did not like the looks of my crew. For some reason, they decided to give us a hard time. My friends and I would get shoved by one of them on the dance floor or on our way to the bar. Dirty looks were thrown like daggers, and there were even a few under the breath comments like, "You guys think you're so hot," or "You think you own this place."

Did we think we were hot? Yes, yes, we did. Did we think that we owned that place? Also, yes, and I have no doubt that we walked around with an arrogance that would suggest that. But after many iced teas and a full night of this "mean girl" behavior, I could no longer keep my mouth shut. While both packs of girls were on the dance floor, a heavy, red-haired girl kept purposely bumping and shoving me while her friends egged her on. After a few minutes, I'd had enough of her bullshit. I stopped dancing and turned to her. In my alcohol influenced, unfiltered state, I yelled over the music, "Hey, I'm not sure why you guys don't like me and my friends, or what the issue is, but this is silly. Let me buy you a drink. Oh. . . wait. Sorry, I don't think they serve Slim Fast at the bar."

Bam! I fell back as her fist made direct contact with my face. Then it was on. Her friends jumped in and then my friends jumped in. It was a full-on bar brawl. Somewhere in the middle of everything, I hit Miss Redhead and broke my finger. Eventually, the employees and the manager broke things up. Because we were the regulars and they were wannabes, they were thrown out of the club, and we were given more free drinks. Our bad behavior was not only tolerated; it was rewarded.

My second bar fight was more of a one-on-one fist fight/cat

fight situation. It was carried out in those tight, spandex mini-skirts we sported back in the early 90's, worn with heels, heavy make-up, and big hair held up by a gallon of hairspray. I was trolling with the same crew I always hung out with, but this night, there was a different boxing opponent.

This opponent was legit mentally unstable. I had been messing around with her ex-boyfriend and she did not like that at all. I was not dating him seriously; I just wanted to "play the field." Having a relationship was not even on my radar, so whatever he and I were doing was far from serious. Regardless, before we knuckled up, she began to stalk me and make my life difficult.

One time, she saw my vehicle at her ex's apartment, so she literally parked her car so tight behind mine that I could not leave. Her ex had to drive me to work and then deal with her later to get my car out. Back then, we didn't have cell phones, but we did have pagers to communicate with each other. Somehow, she managed to obtain my pager number, and would constantly send messages at all hours of the night. I had to turn off my pager when I went to bed. She stalked me, followed me around, and was always going over to her ex-boyfriend's apartment to see if I was there. I quickly grew weary of her behavior.

It all came to blows at our favorite hangout. She was there, and we were there, and all night long she told everyone she was going to "kick my ass" when the bar closed down. I did my best to avoid the confrontation, but when she cornered me in the restroom and said, "I'm gonna kick your ass when this club closes," I respond-ed, "Why wait, Bitch? Let's do this right now in the parking lot!"

The entire crowd followed us outside. There was one small detail about this psychopath stalker that I did not know, and wished her ex-boyfriend had told me: she was a champion kick boxer. When I say "champion," I mean she used to compete and win competitions in her age group.

Her first kick came out of nowhere and caught me squarely in the jaw. How she didn't break my jaw, I'll never know. I fell backwards, but because of the adrenaline coursing through me, I barely felt a thing. After that first strike, all the anger and rage I had been stuffing down for almost twenty years spewed forth. I lost my mind. Even with all her kick-boxing trophies, that girl never had a chance.

I don't remember the details, but I do remember that at the end, I had her on the ground. She was facedown on the concrete, and I was beating on her like a mad woman. It took more than one person to pull me off her, even though it was not much of a fight by then. She was injured, and she was done. After that fight, stalker girl left the state to move back home, and I never saw her again.

All these years later, I still feel bad about that fight. I was as-tounded to realize the depths of my anger, and I'm still ashamed—and a little frightened—that I could injure someone to that extent. Like I said, I'm a passive person who doesn't get upset easily. But that night, I lost control.

It wasn't until years later that I realized the toll this fight took on me. It took years to recognize that with this fight, I actually created my own broken bricks to add to my pile of rubbish. In that situation, I am not proud to have been the one on top. In that situation, I let Norman win.

Fun With Mom

With my friends, I had reckless, and on rare occasions, even destructive fun. But when my mom and I would go out or go away for the weekend, it was different. We would just have a lot of silly, harmless, good times. Back when she was celebrating her freedom from Norman and I was sowing my wild oats, we did a lot of crazy stuff together, despite our rather complicated relationship.

Mom and I were always intrigued by the subject of ghosts and spirits, seeing as we have both had supernatural experiences. One weekend, we decided to rent a room in a hotel that gives ghost tours regularly, and is said to be haunted by multiple spirits. I had always wanted to spend the night in one of those rooms in hopes of seeing, hearing, or experiencing something paranormal. My desire to stay there grew even more after one of the episodes of *Ghost Hunters* was filmed there!

We booked a room at this hotel, spent the day shopping in the quaint little town where it was located, and hit a local bar in the evening. After many drinks, we were in full-on party mode, even to the point of getting up on stage, in front of everyone, and singing "Chantilly Lace," complete with all the hand motions.

When we shut the bar down at 2:00 a.m., we were starving. We drove around trying to find a food joint that was still open. We weren't having much luck until we came across a pizza place. The delivery driver was just leaving on his last run. Pulling in next to him, we asked if we could order a pizza, but he said they had just closed. Seeing a pepperoni pizza in his hand, we began negotiating for that pie. We ended up buying it from him at an incredibly inflated price, which meant he got a great tip for that "delivery," but someone didn't get their pizza that night.

Back at the hotel, we weren't quite ready to retire for the evening because we wanted to hunt ghosts. After all, why should we wait for them when we could walk around and spot them ourselves? We didn't have any luck with the supernatural, but I found some tempting stair railings I wanted to slide down. This would have certainly resulted in serious injuries if Mom hadn't stopped me. She found a small, fluffy dog she tried to steal—until I caught her with it under her shirt. I convinced her we should take it back to the sweet, elderly lady we had seen it with earlier. We returned the puppy, went to our room, and crashed. If any ghosts visited us during the night, we were not aware as we slept soundly in our alcohol-induced comas.

The next day, as we were out strolling through the streets, a couple exclaimed, "You're the duo from last night that sang 'Chantilly Lace'! You guys were so good!" I guess that was my fifteen minutes of fame that everyone talks about. Somewhat lackluster, but nevertheless, we had our first fans!

This little town with the haunted hotel quickly became one of Mom's and my favorite get-aways. Nestled beside a lovely lake in the heart of the Ozark Mountains, it was only about an hour away from where we lived. We loved the beauty of the town and its vibe. Its winding streets, filled with Victorian-style cottages and manors, drew tourists from miles around.

Little did I know that this quaint little town, the sight of so many fun times with my mom, would also be the setting for some of my most humiliating and degrading experiences. But those wouldn't occur until after I was almost killed—again.

TWELVE

The Wreck

"From every wound there is a scar, and every scar tells a story. A story that says, "I survived."

Craig Scott

You would think that I would have the date of a near fatal accident carved into my memory, but by this point, I had added so many traumas to my resumé that all the dates were starting to get muddied. I think the year was 1992, or maybe '93, but I am certain that it was the month of November. I know this because I had a turkey in my refrigerator that I had received from work. When I finally recovered enough from my wreck to go home, that turkey was still in the refrigerator, and it was rotten—like decomposing maggots kind of rotten. You don't quickly forget the sight and smell of something like that!

One thing I do remember about the night of the accident was how chilly it was outside when I cracked the window of my car, hoping the cold slapping me in the face would keep me awake. I was literally minutes from home, less than a mile, and I was desperately trying not to fall asleep at the wheel. Since this would be my week to have my son with me, I needed to get home and get some rest before I went to pick him up.

I had spent the entire weekend celebrating a birthday with my friends. I had gotten into an argument over a boy with one of these friends, so instead of sleeping at her house, as we had planned, I chose to drive home. Seeing as I had barely slept in the previous forty-eight hours, this was not a wise decision.

I remember almost nodding off a couple times and telling myself, "Stay awake, you're almost home." The radio was blaring and the air coming through my half-cracked window was brisk, but not brisk enough to keep me awake. I nodded off for a moment, and when I woke, all I saw was a sharp corner in the road looming in front of me. The last thought I had was, "There's no time to brake!" since I was driving at a significant speed, trying to get home quickly. I covered my face with my hands and braced for impact. As I missed the bend in the road and hit the ditch, my car launched into the air. The only other memory I have is that, at some point, I was screaming in pain. I cannot recall if that was at the accident site or on the way to the hospital. Then I woke up in the ICU.

Remember when I mentioned angels earlier? Well, this was another time when I know they rescued me.

When I missed the turn, my Camaro hit the ditch, causing it to pop up, clear a barbed wire fence, fly into a tree, and then smash into a mobile home. I was not wearing a seat belt, which probably saved my life, because when my car hit that tree, it was ripped almost entirely in half. I had somehow been thrown from the car, and even though I was seriously injured, I was not torn in half along with my seat.

My left arm caught the barbed wire fence on the way down, and I have some nice scars on my arm from that. I had multiple broken ribs on my right side, a collapsed lung, and my liver was shredded from the broken ribs. I was bleeding internally and needed emergency surgery. That's right. On top of the one traumatizing surgical scar that wrapped around the left side of my body, I would now have a scar that went all the way up my stomach.

The unexplainable part of this story is that the paramedics had no idea how I was thrown from the car. My Camaro's T-tops were still securely locked and in place. The window was rolled down part way, but not enough for a body to fit through. Somehow, I had been ejected before the car crashed into the mobile home. My mom said the paramedics told her it was as if an angel had removed me from that car and set me aside. My life was spared, again, through what I consider to be another miracle.

Luckily, the people in the mobile home were not hurt. They were asleep in their bedroom when my car went through their living room. Another God deal if you ask me. Being the only one injured in this accident is one of the many things in my life for which I am extremely grateful. It would have been hard to live with myself if I had hurt or killed someone because of my stupid decision to drive that night.

I was in the hospital about three weeks before being released into my grandparents' care. Because my body was swollen and still in shock, I could barely move. I could not even lift my legs to take a step. It was so bad that, at one point, when I was attempting to use a walker at the hospital, my mom actually had to slip her feet under mine, from behind, and lift our feet together to get my legs to move. I was convinced I would never walk again, and that the doctors just didn't want to give me this news. They kept reassuring me that my body had just suffered a severe trauma due to the impact and internal damage and that I would heal in time. Still, I did not believe them. But since I was ready to get out of the hospital, I quit arguing.

My recovery was slow, painful, and frustrating, even though my grandparents took good care of me and made sure I had everything I needed. They accommodated the special diet I was on because of the liver damage. Since I could not move when I first got to their house, they would roll me over so I wouldn't get bedsores. They also had to help me use the bathroom. Being this incapacitated was a major source of frustration during my recovery.

Another source of frustration was that my ex-husband, Peter, only brought my son to see me once during my recovery. We were supposed to have joint custody. But instead of Peter raising our boy, he allowed his mother, who lived over an hour away, to take him. I was desperate to see my son, but there was nothing more I could do until I had recovered enough to drive and to find another vehicle.

I did not have a lot of visitors during my recovery. I think it was too hard for my friends to see me in the shape I was in. After all, seeing me might have challenged them to face their own demons and decisions.

I do remember my mom visiting. She was always there for me, throughout each traumatic experience I had, no matter what. Even though I would lash out at her from time to time, and even though I kept rebelling and driving myself into the ground, she was always there to pick up the pieces. It wasn't the healthiest of relationships, as she enabled me way too much. Maybe she was trying to make up for the past, for the fact that, for whatever reason, she could not save us from our monster. I did not appreciate her being by my side back then, but I realize now—in this very moment, as I write these words—that I could not have gotten through my life without her.

Collateral Damage

Trying to recover physically wasn't the only hardship I faced in the year following the accident. During that time, the challenges I had been experiencing around transportation, finances, and seeing my son just snowballed. Fallout from the wreck, plus continued bad choices on my part, also created a rift between me and my grandparents.

Initially, I was content being at my grandparents, especially since I spent most of my time drugged up and sleeping. It was a much-needed break from the chaos I had created that was my life. But after living with them for a few months, I had recovered enough to be antsy. As soon as I was able to walk with a cane, I left their care. I told myself that I was leaving because I wanted to see my friends and I missed hanging out with them. But I don't think that was it. Looking back, I realize that at that time, I was in self-destruct mode; I just couldn't help myself. I now know that I should have stayed in this safe place where I was being well cared for. My grandparents knew this back then. That's why they were furious with me when I left.

After moving out of my grandparents and in with a close friend, one of the first things I decided to do was get a tattoo to commemorate that I had survived. Back in the early '90s, ankle tattoos had become popular, along with barbed wire tattoos. I decided that barbed wire wrapping around my ankle would be perfect seeing as the barbed wire fence I grazed when I was thrown from my car had given me a couple of nasty scars on my left arm. To this design I added a crash dummy's head with the words "no fear" written across its forehead. Thirty years later, you can barely make out what the weird head thing is, and the words are no longer legible. But it looked edgy and cool when I first had it done.

For my grandparents, that tattoo was the straw that broke the camel's back. The first time they saw it was at my mom's house, where we had all gathered for Easter dinner. My grandma, bless her heart, said, "That's not permanent, is it? It's one of those stick-on tattoos, right?" I was honest and explained to her that it was not a sticker and that it was indeed a permanent fixture on my body. My grandparents were so upset that they abruptly stood up from the table and left. Maybe they saw this tattoo as another symbol of my continued self-destruction, and they could not bear to witness it. Maybe they were just old-fashioned and narrow-minded. Regardless of the reason, it was at least a year before they would allow me back in their presence, and I had to make sure my tattoo was covered up so as to not set them off again. I have to confess, it was a disappointment to discover that I had to endure rejection from those closest to me when I took a step towards self-love by getting this tattoo to honor my resiliency.

Along with creating a temporary rift between me and my

grandparents, the accident also created some serious transportation problems for me. To start with, even when I was physically able to drive, I was terrified to do so. I did not realize it then, but I was most likely suffering from accident-related PTSD. My fear of driving meant that, for at least a year after the wreck, I had to find people to either take me to visit my son or go pick him up for me. This was a huge ask since he was now living over an hour away at his grandmother's house.

On top of my PTSD, my transportation problems were exacerbated by the fact that my car had been totaled in the wreck. Of course, I had no insurance, because I wasn't able to afford it. I had gone back to work, and was desperately trying to find a way to buy a vehicle. Then, Norman came out of the woodwork saying he wanted to have a relationship with me and he wanted to help me out. I was not interested in having any sort of relationship with my childhood monster, but I did think that, after everything he put us through, he should do something to help me. It was selfish thinking, but I wasn't about to turn away any assistance.

Norman had a truck that he let me borrow for a short time. When he needed it back, he said he was going to take me car shopping, and co-sign on a loan for me, and maybe even help pay for the car. I was shocked and relieved at the same time. I did feel guilty for letting a man that I hated so much do this for me. I felt guilty that I had wished him dead my entire childhood. But my need to survive and get back on my feet managed to override those guilty feelings.

Norman took me to a dealership to look at new trucks because the smaller ones were cheap and special financing was being offered on them. I was excited at the thought of a new vehicle because all I ever drove were hoopties. Having reliable transportation meant everything to me at that point. It would mean that I could see my son more. It also meant that I would not have to worry about making it to work, or breaking down, or being stranded, all of which I had experienced numerous times.

My stepfather and I picked out a truck. We worked with a salesperson to see what financing would be available. The car payment was cheap enough that I felt like I could make it okay on what little I was earning. But Norman would have to take out the loan. I did not have any credit, and I was on the verge of bankruptcy because of all the medical bills from the wreck. The two men were close to coming to an agreement when my stepdad pulled me aside and told me he was backing out of the deal. Norman said he was not comfortable taking out the loan because he did not trust me to make the payments. Not only that, but he said wasn't going to allow me to use his truck anymore. So not only was he not going to help me, but he took away the only transportation I had. I was absolutely crushed. All I could do was cry.

That was the last time I ever spoke to my stepfather.

I had nowhere to go but back to my mom for help. She took me to a place where she knew I could afford to buy a car, a rundown dealership with lots and lots of hoopties. This was fine with me because I was used to driving clunkers. I was just happy to have wheels again. I picked out a brown Mustang that looked like it should have been retired in a junk yard, but the payments were next to nothing.

I had that car for just a few months before it finally died on the side of the road. I called the dealership, told them where the car was, and that they needed to pick it up. I was done with it. That might have been when Mom gave me her hand-me-down car and got another vehicle for herself. Honestly, I went through so many cars that I cannot remember what order they came in or what vehicle I was driving during certain periods of my life. Such were my transportation woes—challenges that only got worse with my accident.

A few months after my wreck, the bills started coming in. I did not have health insurance at the time of the wreck because I could not afford it. The medical bills were staggering, and I could not even make payments against the balance. The hospital ended up garnishing my wages, so I was forced to file for bankruptcy. I did not own a home at the time, so the only property I had was my worn-out Mustang. I decided to throw all my outstanding bills into the bankruptcy; do a complete wipe down. I was ashamed to have to go this route, but I saw no other way out of my financial hole. It was a humbling experience, and it was embarrassing, but I did it, and moved on.

My financial situation, my transportation issues and my relationship with my grandparents were not the only collateral damage from my accident; my relationship with my son had become almost non-existent. I know I am partly responsible for that because my poor choices contributed to this development. The distance between where he and I resided, and the gaps in visitation after my wreck, put a strain on our relationship. He was still so young, a toddler, and probably very confused about his mommy's absences. I was nowhere near being able to fight for custody yet, so the best

I could do was fight my ex-mother-in-law for visitation.

I was determined not to allow this situation to go on forever. I could not be without my son. I was going to fight for him, but it would take a couple more years before I was stable enough to have the funds to hire a lawyer and take this matter to court.

THIRTEEN

Humiliation and Degradation

"I am so much more than you told me I was."
– HealthyPlace.com

All I wanted to do after my car accident was get back out in the world with my friends, live in the bars, bury my feelings, numb my body, and fill my mind with anything but quiet thoughts. When I was drinking and filling my mind with the noise of friends and partying, I didn't have to think about just how broken I felt inside. I didn't have to feel how angry I was about what I *didn't* have—money, transportation, and a way to see my son—and what I *did* have—yet another massive scar on my body. I already thought that my first scar made me less of a woman. Now that I had two, I was certain no man would ever want someone who looked like a carved-up jack-o-lantern. If I slowed down, I would be forced to sit with my own life. I would be forced to deal with it. And I wasn't ready to deal with it yet.

I truly believe God was trying to get my attention with the

accident, but He must have miscalculated the depth of my stub-bornness. Sure, the accident slowed me down physically, for a while, and provided me with a brief wake-up call regarding my recklessness. But it was just that: brief. The reality was that until I fixed my head—my thinking—and until I healed my heart, I was going to continue to follow the same patterns and make the same mistakes. It was inevitable. Abuse and self-deprecation were all I knew. And because these were all I knew, Gerald came into my life.

Gerald

Gerald had a more negative impact on my life than any other person, including my stepfather. He damaged me almost to a point of no repair. For a two-year period, this sadistic alcoholic, along with his equally abusive and inebriated family, degraded me in ways that are absolutely gut-wrenching for me to look back on, even now. These things almost feel like they happened to someone else and not to me. The person I am today does not understand how that girl could have allowed people to be so cruel and in-human to her. It makes me so sad. I can't help but shed tears as I bring up these memories from a very sacred, protected place. I just hope I can do them justice as I move my memories to paper.

I'll never forget the night I met Gerald. It was about a year after my accident, when I was still in my early twenties. My mom and I were spending a weekend away at our favorite little Victo-rian town that was about an hour from where we lived. We were standing on chairs at the back of a packed bar, listening to the live band. That's when I saw him. Gerald was standing at the bar, smiling, and looking right at me. He was older than me (ten years, I later learned), handsome, well-dressed, well-spoken, and I could tell he probably made a lot of money. There was something about his presence, his smile, and his confidence that immediately drew me in.

Gerald made his way over to us, and gave me a pin he had just purchased. It was a brass saxophone that the band must have been selling along with their t-shirts and other paraphernalia. It was a unique gesture. Given my low self-esteem, I wondered why he chose to gift the pin to *me*. At the same time, I was flattered that he was interested in me at all, and giddy at the possibility that I could attract someone of such high caliber. Gerald hung around the rest of the evening, being "Mr. Perfect" and buying me and my mom drink after drink.

If I could go back and change one thing in my life, just one thing, it would be this: I would have never set foot in that bar that night. That one chance meeting drastically impacted the rest of my life in a way that can never be totally healed.

I gave Gerald my contact info that evening, and he called me a few days later to ask me out. I was excited and a bit in shock—a real hot mess! I wasn't sure what a man like this would want with someone like me.

The first night Gerald came over he drove up in a big old Suburban. But this was no ordinary Suburban; this one had been extended and customized. With its blacked-out windows, it looked very impressive sitting next to my hooptie. I immediately felt embarrassed to have Gerald at the house, for him to see where I lived and what I drove. At the time, I was living with my little brother, and he too was taken aback by the older gentlemen that came calling on his big sister.

For our first date, Gerald took me out for dinner and drinks, and then dropped me off at a decent hour. There was one red flag on that date. I saw it, questioned it in my head, and then chose to ignore it. On the way home, Gerald stopped at a liquor store and bought beer—which he proceeded to drink while he was driving. And he didn't drink just one can; he powered through several in a very short time. But like I said, I brushed this off and decided it was no big deal.

I also thought nothing of the early drop off, other than that it was nice to be with a gentleman who showed me the respect of not trying anything funny on the first date. Later I learned that the real reason he dropped me off early was because he was still dating someone back in that quaint little town where we met. He was trying to squeeze in two dates in one night. Gerald eventually came clean about the other woman. That is, he told me that he was trying to break up with her, but that she kept stalking him, and insisting that they were not going to break up.

This situation with the other woman would have been acceptable if we had agreed to see other people, but Gerald made it very clear he did not want me to see other men.

Early on in our courtship, he was late for a date because this other girlfriend came over with a meal she had prepared for him. Gerald said he could not possibly turn down the meal since she had spent so much time working on it. That's why he stayed and ate with her before coming to pick me up. And I let him.

I let him! That was the moment I communicated to him, and to myself, that I was not worthy of anything better. That was the first time I silently gave him permission to treat me poorly. I was so scared he was going to break up with me that I allowed such disrespectful behavior. Trust me when I say that I own a piece of this. But at the time, I did not have a high enough self-esteem or the courage to stand up for my worth as a woman or as a human being.

Gerald's abuse came on as a slow build. He was methodical, and I have learned that this is common among abusers. It's like they all read the same instruction manual or learn how to manipulate and control from some sort of *Abusers 101* training. They slowly start beating you down mentally. They slowly isolate you from your friends and family, and once they get you worn down and alone, the physical abuse begins. Gerald was no different; he followed the program flawlessly.

Like many abusers, Gerald was very charming and pleasant when he was sober. The problem was, he was rarely sober. When he drank, the ugly came out, and it came out with a vengeance. He eased me into the abuse with a few comments here and there about my appearance or my failures as a mother. Gerald liked to pick on certain aspects of my body, kindly letting me know the ways that I did not measure up to other women in his life. He'd make passive aggressive comments at first, suggesting that if I didn't do something about my appearance, if I wasn't perfect, he would be forced to stray. Instead of me leaving the relationship, I poured all my energy into trying to please him. I wanted to be enough. I wanted him to tell me I was enough. He never did, no matter what I tried to change.

Gerald began calling me "Frankenstein" because of my two

large surgery scars. Somewhere along the way, I succumbed to the routine of being weighed weekly and having my waist measured to ensure I was not gaining weight. To put this in perspective, I was five foot nine and only weighed about 125 pounds. I was thin as a rail—too skinny really. My waist was maybe twenty-four inches at its thickest. I was blonde, very young, very thin, and had no reason to be self-conscious. But his daily remarks chipped away at my already fragile self-esteem, slowly prepping me for his physical assaults.

The physical abuse started with an occasional grab of the arm in public if Gerald felt I was being disrespectful or out of line. When we got home, the punishment for my "bad" behavior began to escalate into slapping, locking me in the bathroom, shoving, throwing objects at me, and even some hair pulling from time to time. If his family was present, they would typically join in the fun. His family was just as abusive as he was. They were an incredibly sick and dysfunctional unit.

At some point in the relationship, my mom needed to sell the rental house where my brother and I had been living, so I moved into an apartment of my own. I was at a very, very low point in my life. All I had in the apartment were my bed and a dresser, a few dishes and a couple of towels. That's it. My son would sleep with me when he was over. Since the living room was empty, that became his play area. I contemplated applying for food stamps, but I was too proud to do it, even though I was barely making minimum wage and hardly getting by.

I was in a sad and lonely place, mentally and physically. Conditions were ripe for Gerald to continue to worm his way into my life and brainwash my thoughts. He would come over occasionally and sometimes force himself on me sexually, even if I did not want to have sex with him. He was always drunk when he did this, or on the verge of being drunk. With most abusers, there is always an apology waiting the next day, sometimes with gifts and a promise to do better. But with Gerald, while there were often trinkets for gifts, there was rarely a promise to do better, and even the apologies disappeared over time.

One night, he came over and asked if I would help him wrap Christmas gifts he had bought for his two sons. I agreed, of course, trying to be the dutiful girlfriend. I ended up wrapping them all by myself as he watched, and criticized, and drank. When I was done, Gerald wanted to have sex, but I was on my period and refused his advances. He did not like being told "no." He did not like not getting what he wanted.

In his mind, I needed to be punished for my defiance, so he walked over to the sink that was full of dirty dishes and started with a little verbal foreplay before the big finale. He told me I was a "disgusting pig." That one was his favorite put downs. He used the example of the dirty dishes to remind me that I should not have my son full time because my apartment was disgusting, and I was disgusting, and that my son deserved better. Other than the dishes in the sink, my apartment was spotless, but he still managed to get me to accept as true this alternate reality he was creating for me.

When Gerald grew weary of the verbal assaults, he proceeded to urinate all over my dishes. He told me this was a just punishment for not having them clean in the first place. He then forced me to wash the urine covered dishes while he stood over me and watched. I began to cry, mostly because of the shame and partly because I was just so exhausted from this relationship. I wanted more for myself but did not believe in myself enough to do anything different.

Once the dishes were washed, he had his way with me, period or not. This time I did not fight his advances as I had nothing left by that point in the evening. I shut my mind down and pretended I was somewhere else, somewhere peaceful that made me happy.

When Gerald was done taking what I thought was the last bit of my dignity, he managed to go one step further and completely degrade me as a human being. He took from me what he could and smeared it all over my kitchen cupboards and counters and insisted that I clean that up as well.

Even now, this is horrifying for me to write about. In fact, this part of my story is still so disturbing to me that I almost didn't put it into this book. But after much contemplation, I realized I needed to include this incident to give a full picture of just how inhumanely I was treated, and what I allowed myself to be subjected to.

Many, many more broken bricks. "Thank you, sir. May I have another?"

Hooters

Gerald lived about an hour away from me, in that quaint little tourist town where my mom and I met him. Nevertheless, he frequented the area where I lived for the night life and the women. When he would visit me at my apartment, it was typically on his way to Hooters or on his way home from there, seeing as he was sleeping with at least four of the Hooter girls.

I knew what he was doing, but I just stood by while he showered his Hooter girls with gifts and attention. In my messed-up mind, I told myself I should be lucky that he wanted to grace me with his presence at all. I told myself I should be thrilled to be in such good company as the Hooters girls. Hooter girls wore orange short shorts, and tight, white, low-cut tops, strategically designed to make their cleavage spill out. Back in the day, they were coveted by all the men, and all the women I knew wanted to be them.

Occasionally, Gerald would allow me to go to Hooters with him, or with him and his family. I think it was because he liked to play games with the girls there as much as he liked to mess with me; he liked to show them that they, too, had competition. Gerald was an absolute master at manipulation, always pitting us women against each other. Having me with him worked like a charm for Gerald because my being there drove those girls batty. They made no attempt to be pleasant to me, and would throw themselves at him, pushing me out of the way, even pushing each other out of the way. It's like we were back in high school.

Gerald must have given one of the Hooter girls my pager number because they started harassing me using codes with the pager. I am extremely grateful that cell phones and social media did not exist back then! I am not sure I would have survived that kind of public, consistent, in-your-face bullying. I was in such a fragile state that I would have most likely just withered away into nothing.

One time, Gerald decided he was going to throw a party for the Hooter girls. He spared no expense when it came to these disgusting "ego fests" he used to organize. Gerald called it an "appreciation party," but like always, it was about him and his very large ego. Of course, his mom and uncle were there, and all his favorite Hooter girls. He was footing the bill for a ridiculous amount of alcohol and appetizers and probably feeding some of the other "regulars." He bought the girls gifts and flowers. He loved to show off his money, and he loved to be loved.

I was told that I was not allowed to attend. I was told that the girls did not like me and I would ruin the party if I was there. I wasn't just told; I was threatened. Gerald said, "Do not make me angry by defying me."

It's not like I wanted to go and witness his pathetic, narcissistic behavior. It's not like I wanted to watch the girls fight for his attention while he drank himself stupid. But something in me snapped when he forbade me to go into a public place. I think this was significant for me in that it was the first time I pushed back against him. It was the first time I did not accept being treated like unwanted rubbish.

My plan was not to go to Hooters to join Gerald's party, or even to sit with him and his family. No, I was going to go and see my friend, who was the manager there. I was going to go and show them that they could not control me, that I was not their punching bag. I was fed up with the girls as well, and I wanted to prove a point. I was going to get all dolled up and go there alone. I was afraid, but I did it anyway.

I remember physically shaking as I pulled up to Hooters. I questioned why I was even there. I started my car up twice to leave, only to turn it off again. With every bit of courage I could muster, I slowly got out of my car and walked even more slowly through those forbidden restaurant doors. As I moved around the tables, working my way up to the front counter, I ignored the festivities, the flowers, the music, the gifts he had bought for the girls, and the free food. I sat down at the counter and began conversing with my friend, who was very surprised to see me.

I pretended like I did not even know the family that was obviously in charge that night. I had numerous men ask if I was a Hooter's girl. There was even a table full of slightly intoxicated men that wanted to take a picture with me. I know it sounds silly, but that made my night. It lifted my spirits to know that there were some people who didn't think I was a "disgusting pig," who didn't think I looked like Frankenstein. I am embarrassed to say that I enjoyed the attention. I was having a good time—for about ten minutes. That's how long it was until Gerald's ego couldn't take it any longer.

He came up to me, grabbed my arm, and insisted that I come back to the table where he and his family were sitting. He more than insisted; he dragged me over there. I didn't fight because I was pleased with myself that I had triggered him. But that small shred of confidence and self-love I was experiencing that night quickly vanished as Gerald and his family began to tear into me with their mob-like verbal assaults. The place was packed, people were staring, the girls were laughing, and I started crying. I really, really did not want to cry or show any sort of weakness, but it was just too much. I could not hold back the tears. It wasn't the insults being hurled that broke me that night; I'd heard them all before. It was the humiliation of knowing that other people were now witnessing the madness of my life. It was the realization that I did not love myself enough to stop the degradation.

The mocking, and laughing, and tears created such a pathetic sight that a couple of men jumped in to rescue me. Gerald did not put up a fight or cause a scene when they escorted me away from the table. He was most likely bored of me and ready to get back to his party. The guys walked me out the back and told me they were friends of my brother. They said they could not sit back and watch what was going on any longer because they knew my brother would want them to step in. They asked if I was okay and if I had a ride home. After I calmed down and thanked them for being so kind, they walked me to my car.

I had conceded. Gerald and his family had won. I was going home defeated.

You would think that after that ordeal I would never have gone back to Gerald. But I did. By this time, my wall of shame was so high I did not know how to climb over it. I had let it grow so big that I was not sure how to tear it down and free myself.

Vegas

By this point in the relationship, while I could not figure out how to free myself, I had gotten very good at lying to myself. That's why I was so excited when I was informed that I was going to Las Vegas for the weekend. (I was informed; I didn't have a choice. As with everything else, Gerald made this decision for me.) Gerald said he was going to foot the bill for everything, and I naively thought it was going to be a great trip. I lied to myself about how much fun I was going to have. It was the first time I had ever been to Vegas, and I loved playing slot machines, so why wouldn't I have a great time? Even as I write this, I shake my head at that young girl I no longer recognize and think to myself, "Bless her heart." Of course that trip was going to be a disaster! A womanizing drunk in Vegas? Stuff was bound to go wrong!

We didn't even make it through the plane ride before things got sketchy. From the start of his drinking—which commenced before 8:00 a.m.—to his non-stop flirting with the flight attendants, to him insisting that we become part of the "mile high club," I was already tired of Gerald and his behavior before we even landed in Sin City. By the time we arrived at our hotel, he was already drunk. That's when I knew it was going to be a very, very long weekend.

We spent most of the day at the casino where Gerald was on a winning streak. He gave me coins to keep me occupied while he did whatever he wanted. I was happy with that. I didn't win much, but I was content to be by myself for a few hours. Because Gerald was spending so much and winning so much, we got our meals comped. I ate very well that weekend and we had a fantastic suite.

By the time night hit, Gerald was smashed, but he had a pocket full of cash. He wanted to hit the strip bars and dance clubs. Me? I was tired. And I was angry that he would not allow me to retire to our lovely suite. Instead, he insisted that I accompany him. Being in those strip clubs was humiliating for me, especially since I struggled deeply with my own body image. The way he drooled all over those naked women made me feel so incredibly insignificant. I remember looking at my own body later that night and pointing out to myself every single flaw I had. I absolutely hated myself.

That's how the weekend went. And that's how Vegas became

yet another place that Gerald ruined for me. Just like Hooters, I can never go there now without thinking about all the degrading things I experienced while I was there with him.

The Resort

Gerald made his money from a luxury lakeside resort he had built in that tourist town where he and I met. Knowing that I was barely staying afloat financially, he came to me one day and offered me a resort manager position that seemed way too good to pass up. The job would require me to live onsite. This was not a problem seeing as the manager's lodge accommodations were incredible! The place was all decked out, and even had a hot tub on the balcony overlooking the lake. I could live in this beautiful place and have no bills except my food. The arrangement outlined to me was that I would stay onsite Monday through Friday and tend to the customer's needs, take reservations, and make sure the cleaning ladies did what they were supposed to do. My nights would be free, unless I had to help a customer or take calls. I would also have the weekends off, and could leave the resort on weekends and week nights.

The plan was that I would come home Friday nights and stay with my mom until Sunday afternoon. The pay was more than I had ever made, and because I was not spending hardly any money, I could start saving for the legal battle I knew was in my immediate future. At this point, I was only seeing my son every other weekend. He was still living with his grandmother, and she rarely let me have him. At least now I could pick him up and keep him longer because I had a nice place for him to stay and enough money to care for him. Little did I know that this "dream job" would quickly become a veritable hostage situation.

I enjoyed the job initially. It wasn't difficult, I had everything I needed, and I was surrounded by breathtaking scenery every day. For the first time, I felt like maybe I could save enough money to get my life together, which for me, meant secretly finding a place of my own and maybe a different job back home.

The weeks I had my son at the lodge were some of our best times. They were also very peaceful. Gerald and his family were busy with the resort, so they mostly left me alone those weeks. Of course, one of them would regularly check in on me to make sure I was staying at the lodge, not leaving the grounds, and not having any guys over. Other than that, it was a relatively safe place for me, especially seeing as, because of their customers, none of the family drank as much on the property.

It was a sweet deal in the beginning, but the challenges around trying to leave through the week quickly began to wear on me. I had thought I would at least be able to leave in the evenings and have some free time. But that could only happen if Gerald approved it, and if someone was available to stay at the resort in my place in case one of the customers needed something. Gerald allowed this once or twice in the beginning, but getting his permission—which required explaining why I needed to leave the resort—was such an ordeal that it quickly became not worth the effort. As the isolation of the resort became harder than I had anticipated, I grew increasingly homesick. That's why I really looked forward to the weekends. Unfortunately, I only left the resort during a few weekends before Gerald took that privilege away too.

Hot Springs, Missed Races, and Chocolate Pie

During a weekend that I was able to leave the resort, my mom and I had one of our fun, silly adventures. We decided to make an overnight trip out of driving to Hot Springs for the horse races. We were super excited as we packed up our car and headed out of town. When we arrived at our destination, some three- to four-hours later, we were a bit concerned that the town looked so dead on a race day. We pulled into the parking lot of the race grounds where there was not another car in sight. Surely people would start filtering in for the races soon, we thought. Brushing it off, we went to check in to our motel, deciding that we would come back closer to race time. But when we asked the clerk at the front desk why the town was so empty on race day, they explained that we had come on the wrong day!

Well, since we were already there, Mom and I decided to make the best of it. We spent the day gambling away our money at the slot machines of the town's small casino, making our coins last as long as possible. From there, we headed to the local bar, where a couple of gentlemen tried their best to hook up with us. That certainly wasn't going to happen, but Mom and I were happy to down the drinks they sent our way. We danced with them, and did some shots, and generally had a good time.

By the time we left the bar, I was smashed. Mom was driving, and I insisted I needed a piece of chocolate pie. I was drunk, and hungry, and would not shut up about it. Attempting to appease my unconventional request, Mom stopped at a Waffle House so we could get my damn chocolate pie, which we ended up taking to go.

When we arrived back at our room, the key did not work. It was one of those strip hotels where the rooms were lined up and the entrances were outside. We kept fussing and fussing with the key in the lock until a very big, very groggy, and very shaggy man threw open the door. Shaggy man was in his underwear and did not look happy!

We were not happy that this man was in our room. "What the hell are you doing in our hotel room?" I shouted. Confused, we finally looked around and realized that we were at the wrong hotel altogether! We took off, laughing uncontrollably. Eventually, Mom managed to find the right hotel and get us into our room.

I sat down at the little table to eat my chocolate pie. After my pie, I lit a cigarette, because when you're a smoker, you must smoke after you eat. It's like an unwritten rule. As I was sitting there smoking, we discussed the mishaps of our day. I began laughing so hard that I fell over in the chair and onto my lit cigarette, burning my back. After finishing my now smashed cigarette, I finally passed out in bed.

Mom and I were having so much fun all weekend that I chose not to answer Gerald's call or return his pages. I just needed a break. I needed to unplug. I needed to pretend that my life was different than it was.

When I got back to the resort, Gerald demanded that I stop by his house before I went to the lodge. He was hammered and angry. We fought over me leaving and not staying in contact with him. When Gerald saw the cigarette burn on my back, he pressed me for information on how that happened. I told him the story of me falling off the chair, but he didn't believe me. Gerald punched me in the eye, which quickly turned black. I snapped, went into his bedroom, and grabbed his boy's BB gun, intending to pummel him with BBs. Gerald overpowered me and took the weapon away. He then picked me up, carried me outside, and threw me onto the pavement. That weekend was the most banged up I ever got during those two years.

When I went home the following weekend and my mom saw my eye, I thought she was going to lose her mind. She told my brother's and they threatened to drive up and "kick his ass." I begged them all to leave it alone. I was not yet prepared to endure the repercussions from Gerald or his family that such actions might have. I was too scared to walk away.

Practically a Hostage

Gerald did not like the idea of having no control over what I did when I was out of his reach, so soon after that weekend away with my mom, I was not allowed to leave the resort unless it was with him. He told me if I left, I would be fired. Then he came up with new weekend responsibilities for me. I was put to work as a cleaning lady and ended up working six or seven days a week.

During this period, I was certain he had other love interests who kept him occupied, since I only saw him a few days a week. But getting some breaks from being Gerald's and his family's target was actually a relief to me, especially seeing as his family was as abusive as he was. One night we were all at Gerald's house. I had gone to bed while they continued to drink themselves into oblivion. While I was sleeping, his mother barged into the bedroom, grabbed me by my hair, dragged me out of bed, and into the living room. She then threw me to the ground in front of her son and made me kneel, as if I was before a king. She proceeded to scream at me about how disrespectful I was to him and that I needed to start responding to him with, "Yes sir" and, "No sir."

It's no wonder I didn't care who Gerald was sleeping with or what he did anymore as long as he and his family left me alone.

As I began to feel more and more like I was being held hostage by Gerald and his family, my mom and my brothers became increasingly worried about me. There were times when I tried to plan an escape, but I was always too terrified to leave. My mom visited the lodge at least twice to try and pull me out of the situation. Each time she came to visit, Gerald would become irate, and I would suffer the consequences. One night after she left, he came to the manager's lodge, drunk and pissed off. He dragged me to the hot tub on the balcony, held my head under the water, pulled me up to yell at me, then pushed my head back under. He did this over, and over, and over again until he finally got bored with his game.

My First Turning Point: Divine Intervention

After two years of mental and physical abuse, of degradation and humiliation, of being brainwashed and broken down, I was just a shell of a person. I had shut down. I had given up. I had accepted my fate: either they were going to do me in, or else I would end it myself with a bottle of pills.

But one day, something totally unexpected happened—something I can only describe as a miracle.

There was nothing special about this day; nothing out of the ordinary horror. Gerald had just returned from one of his many trips. As was expected during his absences, I had been babysitting his two young sons, cleaning his resort, cleaning his house, and dealing with his drunken family. Having finally finished my Cinderella chores, I took his boys fishing, down at Gerald's boat dock, thinking it would be nice to get some fresh air. He arrived at the dock with his entourage—his intoxicated uncle and his inebriated, enabling mother—and proceeded to lecture me on how I had not cleaned his house to his specifications.

Then the beers came out of the coolers (they never traveled anywhere without full coolers of beer) and the family drank themselves into their typical frenzy. Such frenzies involved ganging up on someone and verbally attacking them without mercy. Since Gerald's boys were always treated like little princes, and I was the only other person there that day, the verbal assaults rained down on me. Again, this was nothing new. I was used to enduring this gang harassment at least once a week.

As they laughed and mocked at my expense, I felt myself begin to shut down and turn off inside. I went into a daze that felt like a near death experience; it almost felt like I was floating above myself and watching what was occurring. Their voices became faint until I no longer heard them.

Then their rants were replaced by a voice I did not recognize. This voice was calming, soothing. It whispered in my ear, "You do not have to endure this any longer. Stand up. Walk away. Go home."

Before when I had wanted to run, I was afraid and unsure. But when I heard this voice, a sense of peace came over me. I had no fear.

I immediately stood up, and without one word, I walked away, got into my car, and drove to my mom's house.

I attribute this voice to my guardian angel. I can think of no other explanation. Something came to my rescue that day and silenced the voices in my head that told me I was not enough; that this is what I deserved. It quieted my fears long enough to give me the courage to walk away. I had tried leaving a few times before, but this was different. Whatever guided me that day gave me the strength to never return. It had to have been my angel. She managed to shut down my fears and fill me with the strength to save myself.

Of course, Gerald did not give me up easily. He attempted to find me, contact me, and stalk me to the point that I left the state for six months. I took a job in Oklahoma so as not to be tempted to return to that abusive situation. I like to think that I would not have gone back even if I had not left the state. But I was so damaged at the end of this relationship that I know I needed that distance to keep me from returning.

PART FOUR

A DECADE OF
DISASTROUS MARRIAGES

FOURTEEN

The Controller

"When a person attempts to control someone else's life,
it only reflects the lack of control they have on their own."

Daniel Chidiac

Leaving Oklahoma and returning to Arkansas, I found employment in the business office of a local newspaper. This was a good job for me because I enjoyed going to work every day and, for the most part, I liked all my co-workers. I was in my late twenties and starting to get my life settled so I could afford to fight for full custody of my son. I felt hopeful about the future, even though I was tattered from my past. I felt there was still time for me to turn my life around. I believed I was not yet damaged beyond repair.

My mom was my only friend at this point. Seeing as I had let Gerald isolate me from all my friends, the gang I used to hang out with was no longer in my life. My mom was single as well, and going through a "sowing her wild oats" period of her own. After being in a miserable relationship with Norman all those years, she could finally do what she wanted. During this time in our lives, we were both experiencing a delayed season of freedom. Unfortunately for me, my freedom was short lived.

Husband #2: Martin

The night I met Martin I was at a local bar with my mom. Martin was there by himself. I never questioned why he was alone in a dark bar with no friends, no date, no one to hang out with. All he had was a table in a dark, quiet corner. Was this a red flag that I missed? Who am I kidding? Even if it was, I would have ignored the flag. I would have grabbed it, wadded it up and discarded it into the commonsense trash can because Martin was attractive, and he seemed interested in me. That's pretty much all it took back in those days.

My mom and I came up with this game to see if he was interested. I'd walk by him to go to the bar or the bathroom, and she'd watch to see if he watched me walk by or turned his head as I passed. We played that game more than once, and more than once he watched me walk by or turned his head. Not too long after that, we invited Martin over to our table for a drink. Not too long after that, Martin and I were dating.

Martin was an intense individual who wanted an intense relationship immediately. Red flag! Red flag ignored. I took it as a compliment. I was flattered by his immediate need to be with me... All. The. Time.

I only noticed a few warning signs with Martin at the beginning, but others slowly appeared while we were dating. I was unsettled by some of his behaviors, and had plenty of time to end the relationship. But once again, I chose to ignore my instincts. I told myself, "It's fine. Everything's fine." Coming out of what I had just endured, if he didn't hit me or verbally assault me, I was happy.

I did not realize that there was another type of abuse I had to watch for—control. I thought it was sweet when Martin came looking for me on my girl's night out. "Oh, look how much he cares about me; he came to find me because he missed me." I thought it was endearing when he wanted me to work at his company after I quit my job at the paper. "Oh, look how much he loves me; he can't stand to be away from me." Like Gerald's abusive behavior, Martin's controlling behavior was a very slow build, so I was truly happy while we were dating and even through the first couple years of our marriage. I didn't push back on the increasingly suffocating behavior as it was way more manageable than the abuse I was used to.

One of the things I appreciated most about Martin was that he encouraged me to work out with him at the gym. Other than a small stint of running track in California, this was my first real introduction to fitness, and I loved it! Martin stood six feet tall and was very muscular; body-building muscular. He worked out quite a bit, lifting weights and trying to bulk up. He liked me to go with him, and I even lifted weights, but the rule was that I was not allowed to look at any other guys. I had to look down most of the time. If Martin even thought I was looking at someone else, he would get angry and threaten to not let me return to the gym.

But like I said, I was content for the first few years of our marriage, even happy. We had my daughter at the beginning of the marriage, so I was busy with being a mom. My daughter had severe asthma as a child and was highly allergic to her surroundings. Her asthma was so bad that we were in the emergency room on a regular basis. If I cleaned the house while she was in it, it would set off her allergies, which in turn, would set off her asthma. By the time she was two, she began getting weekly allergy injections.

Originally, the doctors thought my daughter might have Cystic Fibrosis because she was continually coughing up mucous. The specialist Martin and I took her to discovered that the lining to her airways had become damaged due to pneumonia she had as an infant. The lining never healed because of her asthma attacks, so her body was overproducing mucous. The doctors put her on some experimental drugs and slowly she began to recover. By the time she started kindergarten, her asthma was completely gone.

The Custody Battle

In the middle of my daughter's health issues, Martin and I filed for full custody of my son. After all this time, I was delighted to finally be in a position where I could gain permanent custody. By the time we filed, my son was six years old. My ex-husband, Peter, had remarried. He and I were each at a place in our lives where we could provide a home suitable for our son. The only difference was that Peter didn't really want custody. For all these years, he'd had the opportunity to participate in our joint custody agreement, but he never did. He'd had the opportunity to raise our boy while I was recovering from my accident. This would have kept my son close by so I could see him, but my ex had not taken this opportunity. He had left our son with his mother instead. I was the one that filed for custody. Peter never did. He just wanted to fight it because his mom was adamant about keeping her grandson.

Peter's wife also got involved, and she was relentless. She had my ex call the school and change all the emergency contact information to their info. The two of them got the names of all my son's teachers, fed them their side of the story, and convinced them that I was a horrible mom and that they should help my ex obtain custody. They had the teachers notify them if anything at all was "off" while my son was in my care. I read an email that one teacher wrote to Peter saying they were concerned because my son came to school with a hole in his jeans. Seriously?!? They put me under such a microscope that I felt physically sick and anxious all the time. I questioned my ability as a mother, and second-guessed every parenting decision I made. I was terrified to make a mistake because I knew they would use it against me.

To financially survive the custody battle, Martin and I took a second mortgage out on the house. Not only did we have to pay our attorney, but the judge ordered Peter and I to split the cost of an attorney ad litem for my son. This was an attorney whose sole purpose was to represent my son's best interest in these proceedings. The cost was astronomical, but it was worth every penny.

In the midst of all that was going on with my son's custody case and our daughter's health issues, Martin and I also got full custody of his daughter. Martin's ex-wife was falling off the rails, and we had evidence on her that forced her to sign over custody. Despite how Martin treated me, he was a great father and a good stepfather.

Meanwhile, with my son's case, we went through discoveries and depositions, home studies and meetings with the attorney ad litem. It was a long and exhausting process. In the courtroom, my ex's attorney attempted to paint me as the equivalent of a crack whore who used to be homeless and was not worthy of raising a child. It was that bad. It was also just a lot of smoke and mirrors and untruths.

What it finally came down to for the judge was the fact that, beginning with my car accident. and against my wishes, my ex-husband gave our son to his mom to raise. Peter admitted to the fact that I had asked him not to leave our son at his mother's, but to keep him while I recovered. He admitted that he did not participate in the joint custody agreement for quite some time. Those things were what ultimately led to my winning full custody of my son.

While I was overjoyed with the outcome, this custody battle impacted me greatly. The lack of self-esteem I already experienced was compounded by the allegations my ex-husband desperately hurled to sway the judge's decision and by being watched constantly. These things further contributed to my feelings of low self-worth as a mother. In fact, I doubted myself as a mother for many years after this battle, and I still struggle with these doubts from time to time.

Increasing Control

During the first few years of our marriage, the custody battle for my son and our daughter's health issues took up all my spare time. I did not have time to socialize or do anything other than go to work and take care of my family. Once these things were behind us, I wanted to start going places with my mom or my work friends. I wanted to occasionally go to the gym by myself. This is when Martin's controlling behaviors began to build.

Over time, Martin replaced my friends with his and isolated me from my family. He stopped letting me go out with my mom. He insisted that we spend holidays with his family. We only socialized with joint work friends. For a long time, our colleagues never knew what was going on behind closed doors. As I had done in high school, I compartmentalized my home life and never shared what was going on with our work friends until those last few months when everything unraveled. That's when our coworkers also began seeing changes in Martin because he could no longer hold up the charade.

People can only hide their crazy for so long before it starts to leak out. I still remember the weekend that two girls from work invited me to the lake. One of them had access to a boat, and they were going to do a girl's day out on the water. I wanted to go so badly, but when I asked my warden if I could go, he got very upset. Martin told me that not only was I not allowed to go, but that wearing a bathing suit in public, where other guys could see me, was not an appropriate thing for a wife to do. I remember crying and thinking, "Surely this is not normal." I realized I did not want to live like this, and I believe this realization was the first stepping-stone on the path of me choosing to pursue a divorce.

What made this whole experience even worse was that, on Monday, when we both went to work, Martin yelled at the girls for inviting me. I think this was the first time they recognized that something was not quite right with him.

Near the end of our marriage, there were too many rules to remember. I could not go to a bar without Martin. I could not go to a restaurant, or anywhere else that served alcohol, without him. I could not be in public in a swimsuit without him. I could *never* look at other men, especially at the gym. If Martin allowed me to hang out with my mom or my friends, he followed me. If he couldn't follow me, he would time me to make sure I was driving to the location I said I was visiting. He would then call me throughout the day to check up on me.

Martin monitored my activities in just this way the Mother's Day before it all blew up. He had inquired about what I wanted for a gift, and I asked him if I could spend the day with my mom. We wanted to go hang out in that quaint little town we both liked, the one where I had met Gerald. There was so much to do there, and we enjoyed the shopping, but mostly I just needed a break from the house. I wanted a day to myself where I did not have Martin breathing down my neck every second. He granted my wish, but it was not without control.

Not long after we arrived in that little town, my phone started blowing up. I ignored Martin's calls at first, pissed off that he would not leave me alone. At one point, my mom grabbed my phone and told him to quit calling. He began to argue with her over the fact that he did not believe we were where we said we were. I agreed to speak with him, and he told me that he timed me when I left the house and there's no way I could have arrived at our destination as fast as we did. He thought I was lying and demanded I come home. I refused and told him I would be home later. He continued to call throughout the day, but I ignored his calls because I was fed up with him.

That incident spurred a large argument which resulted in Martin becoming physically violent for the first time. He put his foot through our glass living room table and threatened to kill me if he found out I was having an affair, or if I left him. This was a side of him I had never seen before, and it was scary. In fact, it rattled me so much that I called his mother to come out and calm him down. I should have called the police, but I was scared it might set him off more. It was a mistake to call his mother because she blamed me for his behavior. After calming Martin down and having a discussion with him, she turned to me and asked, "What have you done to upset him like this? Are you having an affair? Why would you talk about leaving him when he's a great dad and a great husband?" I did not know at the time that she had information about his past that would have been useful. I did not know at the time that he had been arrested for domestic violence—not just once, but twice. But still, she blamed me.

FIFTEEN

A Tragic Ending

"One of the reasons a survivor finds it so difficult
to see herself as a victim is that
she has been blamed repeatedly for the abuse.
Each time she is used and trashed,
she becomes further convinced of her innate badness."
–Diane Langberg

My Second Turning Point: A Realization

I had been thinking about leaving Martin for quite some time. Prior to him putting his foot through our glass table, there were several occasions when I had suggested that maybe we consider separating. After two of those conversations, Martin took off with our daughter and then called me, threatening that I'd never see her again if I left him. He said he wasn't going to hurt her, but that he would run away with her. Twice after I mentioned leaving him, he also removed all the funds from our bank account, so I did not have access to any money. Because of his drastic responses, each time, I gave in and stayed.

But it wasn't long before I reached my breaking point. There was no big incident that triggered this. I simply arrived home from work one day and found myself sitting in the driveway, crying, because I didn't want to go inside my house. That's when I realized that I did not have the strength or the mental capacity to continue living the way I was—especially now that Martin's mental health seemed to be slipping. Some days he could not even make it out the door to go to work. He was also becoming erratic and violent. For these reasons, I knew there was a very high probability he would hurt me, kill me, come after me, or harass me—anything but let me go quietly. But this day, I decided that it was okay if he did *all* those things, because I would rather die than continue living in this prison. I had had enough.

Based on my previous experiences of trying to leave Martin, this time, I knew I needed a plan. I had numerous conversations with my mom, planning my finances and my escape. I had numerous conversations with a friend who was a part-time police officer, trying to understand the best course of action. We discussed getting a restraining order, but I knew that it would not stop Martin from coming after me; it would just set him off. Instead, I made the decision to tell Martin I wanted to get a divorce at my mom's, with her present, to try and discourage any violence. I regret that decision to this day.

In the plan I worked out with my mom, I would convince Martin to go visit his family for the weekend and I would take that time to get things in order so I could leave him for good. I would spend the weekend with my mom, or at least be there Sunday when he returned. I hoped that if I could get him to come to my mom's house, and I could tell him I was leaving him with someone present, then the discussion would go somewhat smoothly. My police officer friend had also confirmed that I should definitely not try to talk to Martin when I was alone with him in our home.

In my plan, I arranged to have each of the children spend the weekend with different relatives. What I was not prepared for was Martin's insistence that our daughter go with him to his mom's house. That was the only way he said he would go. He used our daughter as collateral; as a bargaining tool. I had no choice but to agree to his terms.

The other thing I was not aware of was that Martin had worked himself up into a psychotic state while at his mom's, perhaps because I was not taking his incessant calls. Before that weekend, his mental state had become enough of a concern that a mutual work friend suggested marriage counseling when she finally saw how he was behaving. We went one time, but it only made the situation worse. Our marriage counselor told Martin he could not behave in the manner he was; that I was not his prisoner. That one visit occurred shortly before this fateful weekend. In fact, I later learned that Martin had tried to contact the therapist again before that final weekend because he knew he was not in a good place mentally. It is my understanding that the therapist did not get back with him in time to possibly prevent what went down.

A Literal Hostage

It was June 2003, and I was thirty-two years old. I was still so young, but I felt like I had lived a lifetime. I was already so tired, so worn down, and my current situation had come to a boiling point. I was frantic. I was desperate. And, unbeknownst to me, so was Martin. I found out so much after this weekend due to the investigation that was spurred by his family. I found out that he was taking medication that weekend to try and calm himself down. I had not been home all weekend, so I'm not sure what time he arrived back at our house. But after he got home, he called everyone he knew to find out if they had seen or talked to me. He called friends to tell them goodbye. One of the most eerie conversations he had was with our boss; Martin told him he was not going to be working for him anymore.

Martin kept trying to coax me into coming home and talking to him there, but I refused. It's a good thing I didn't go home because, when I finally went back to the house, I found a baseball bat sitting at the front door. I believe that bat was meant for me. We did not own a gun, as I never wanted one in the house with the children. I have no doubt that this decision saved my life because I now believe he meant to kill me.

Martin was not a drinker, but I also found our home littered with empty alcohol bottles. Our van that he drove to my mom's house had a huge, half empty bottle of vodka in it. I am just thankful that my daughter remained safe through all this craziness. So much could have happened to her before I even met with him.

When Martin showed up at my mom's house, I did not even recognize the person standing in the doorway. He was wild-eyed, and not even wearing a shirt. The look on his face was absolutely frightening. My mom immediately grabbed my daughter and took her out in the back yard. We had gone and picked up some lunch for her and it was a nice summer day. Grandma was going to have a picnic with her while mommy and daddy talked.

Martin entered the house and never said a word. I told him we needed to talk, and he never said a word. I asked him where his shirt was, and he never said a word. From there, everything happened so quickly.

We sat on the couch and I just blurted it out. I told Martin I wanted a divorce. It felt like he was ready for it, like he knew exactly what I was going to say. Still, he never uttered a word; he did not make a sound. Martin grabbed me and put one hand over my mouth and tried to put his other hand over my nose. He was trying to quietly smother me with my mom and daughter outside, unaware of what was going on.

There are no words to describe the sheer terror I felt at that moment. My fight or flight instincts kicked in, and I fought like hell. He could not get a firm enough grasp on me to shut off my air, so he aborted that method. When he moved his hand off my mouth, I tried to scream, but he quickly muzzled me again. He then wrapped one of his hands around my hair and dragged me into the kitchen.

When he got me into the kitchen, I wriggled loose just enough to begin screaming as loudly as possible to alert my mom. I did not want her to come into the house, but I wanted her to take my daughter to safety and call the police. Her mama bear instincts must have kicked in, and she came through the kitchen door, leaving my daughter at a safe distance outside.

Once we were in the kitchen, and right before my mom came

through the sliding glass door, Martin began looking around for a weapon. I knew what he was doing, so my eyes began darting around the kitchen as well. We were both looking for the butcher's block, but for very different reasons. Martin found it first, and even with me screaming and fighting him, he managed to maneuver the large butcher's knife out of its block. Now he was armed.

I screamed at my mom to get out of the house and call for help. She ignored my plea and attempted to fight him for the knife instead. This resulted in her getting kicked into the wall. I was grateful that was all he did to her. Once she was down on the floor, I again tried to get him to drop the knife.

At one point during our struggle for the weapon, Martin did drop the knife and my mom dove for it. He managed to kick her again and when he did, I got loose enough to try and grab it myself, but he beat me to it. He was becoming visibly flustered and with knife in hand, he began to drag me down the hall and into the small bathroom that was located by the front door. I remember thinking that I was being dragged to the place where I was going to die. As the thought, "I am going to die today," flashed through my mind, I began to cry. As the dark reality of the situation set in, I became terrified of what was coming next.

That's when my mom finally rushed outside to safety and called the police. She grabbed my four-year-old daughter, who had crept closer and was weeping, because she had seen everything through the glass door. They ran. My daughter tells me that, to this day, she still remembers bits and pieces of what she saw through that door. It's something she will live with for the rest of her life, and it devastates me, as a mother, to know that she has to do this.

Once he dragged me into the bathroom, Martin locked the door and stood in front of it, blocking any chance for my escape. He had me pinned in the corner, up against the sink. He held the knife to my throat and told me over and over that he was going to slit my throat. He was going to kill me because, "If he couldn't have me, no one would." He was rambling on and on about how "I was not going to leave him" and that "he had already been divorced twice before and refused to get another divorce." My whole body was shaking with fear. I was paralyzed. I could not move or speak or cry or think. I lost all track of time. I had no idea how long this went on.

Then the cops arrived. I could hear the sirens out front, and I felt a slight moment of relief. I pictured in my head: the police barging through the door at any moment and saving me, but that never happened.

When Martin realized there were police outside, he began to panic. He told me he was not going to jail. He said that was not an option. All I could think to do was to try and talk him down, try to back him off the ledge. This man was six feet tall with a muscular build. If I thought for a second, that I could fight him for the knife in that tiny bathroom and win, I would have gone for it. But that was a death sentence for sure. It was not possible for me to over-power him. I had nowhere to go. I was trapped.

I found my voice and began telling him anything I thought he wanted to hear. I said I would not leave him, and I promised to stand by him. I told him I wouldn't press charges and that we'd work it out. I begged him not to kill me. I begged for my life. I closed my eyes and said a prayer to any god that would listen. I selfishly prayed that it would not hurt too much, and I prayed for my daughter and my mom to not be harmed.

After a few minutes of incoherent rambling, he then told me he was going to kill himself. He said that was the only way out for him. Being held at knifepoint, I assumed what he meant was, "I'm going to kill you and then I'm going to kill myself." That's what you hear about all the time; the attacker kills his wife and his family and then commits suicide. But apparently, Martin changed his mind about killing me that day. I will never know why he changed his mind. He had been planning it, I am now certain of that, and he was very intent on doing so just moments before. I hold on to the belief that God, or my guardian angel, was there for me once again. I hold on to the belief that they got into his head that day and saved my life.

With a dazed look, Martin turned the knife around on himself. He took a minute to make sure it was positioned right over his heart. Then he kept repositioning and repositioning the knife until he was certain it would do the most damage. I remember hearing that if someone is going to commit suicide, they won't hesitate. The more they hesitate, the less likely they will follow through with it. So I kept talking to him, distracting him, waiting for the police to come in and help. They never came. Maybe they had to wait for back up. I'm not certain. All I knew was that I had never felt more alone in my life. I was alone in that bathroom trying to save my life and, oddly enough, trying to save the life of my attacker.

Martin begged me to push the knife into his heart. I was crying and refused to do so. I told him this was not the answer. As much as I feared him, and even though I knew, if he lived, he would come after me again, all I could think about was my little girl, to whom he was a good father. I was trying to save his life for her. Martin told me he was going to fall on the knife. He glanced around to see if there was room for him to just fall with the knife pointing into his chest. He was mumbling something about "it could miss when he fell on it" and that "it would probably not work."

I continued to try and talk him down. I was certain that so much time had passed that there was no way he would follow through now—especially doing it this way; it was so brutal. I never believed he would turn the knife on himself. I expected him to kill me with it at the last minute and then let the cops shoot him. I honestly believed that's what was getting ready to go down and, once again, I started to pray.

There was a brief instant when I saw the man I used to know. Just a brief moment. The madness left his eyes and was replaced with fear and sadness. I thought at that moment that everything was going to be okay. I thought he was coming to his senses and maybe he would walk out of that bathroom and turn himself in to the police. I was wrong.

With the knife still pointing at his chest, and without warning, Martin let out a scream and then slammed himself into me. It happened so fast I had no time to react. I was still backed up into the corner and up against the sink. The impact drove the butcher's knife deep into his chest and knocked me up against the wall. I remember screaming and the picture on the wall falling off and hitting me. Martin was in shock and I was in shock. He was still standing in front of the door and I was still trapped.

Then it was like Martin woke up and realized what had happened. He frantically tried to pull the knife out of his chest. The look on his face was of disbelief, like he could not believe he had actually done that to himself. As Martin was working on removing the knife, he stepped over by the shower, moving away from the door far enough for me to make a run for it. Unlocking the door, I ran outside and screamed at the police that my husband had stabbed himself and they needed to call an ambulance. Then I sat down on the driveway and cried.

I was in shock. The rest of the day was so foggy that I don't remember many details after that. My neck was red where Martin had tried to smother me, and my chest was red where the handle of the knife had hit when he slammed into me. My head hurt where he had managed to pull out chunks of hair. Once the police got me up on my feet, I ran over to my mom and daughter who were sitting on the lawn. They were also crying. I don't remember reporters being there, but they must have arrived, because the next day I saw my picture in the newspaper. They had taken a picture of me sitting on my mom's lawn while we were waiting for the paramedics to take Martin out of the house on the stretcher. I don't know how many cops were outside, and I don't know how long it took for the ambulance to arrive. I thought Martin was going to live, and I was thankful for my daughter but very afraid for myself.

Due to the nature of the event, we were forced to stay at that house all day while the police did whatever they needed to do to collect evidence and interview us. There was blood everywhere. Martin had impaled himself in the front bathroom. After I escaped, he must have left the bathroom and headed up the hallway, because there was a large trail of blood there. And that's where the para-medics found him, lying on the floor. He had managed to remove the knife, and that was where the largest pool of blood collected.

The blood-stained images of the aftermath still haunt me to this day. The shear amount of blood was horrific.

The police kept my mom and I apart and in separate bedrooms with the doors closed. I was traumatized, and I was alone. I know it was probably protocol, but it seemed especially cruel after what I had just gone through. The police let me call someone to come pick up my daughter, so at least she did not have to endure what we did. My mom had given me a Valium or a Xanax to calm me down, and I just laid on the bed and drifted in and out of sleep for what seemed like hours.

There was a detective in the bedroom with me. He was the one who told me that Martin had died at the hospital. Earlier, before I had heard that news, I asked him how they were going to protect me when my husband got out of jail. He just stared at me and could not provide me with any answers.

My mom and I were finally brought to the police station later that day for more questioning. They asked us for our clothes and one of the cops asked me to take a lie detector test. That was the first inkling I had that I was being treated like a suspect and not like the victim I was. I tried to tell myself that this was common practice since it was just Martin and I in that bathroom and no one witnessed the event. But I was angry. I was not going to take any chances, so I called my lawyer.

Aftermath

When my lawyer arrived at the station, I was finally released and told I could go home. I thought the ordeal was over, but in many ways, it was just beginning. I soon learned that I did not have a penny to my name. Martin had cleaned out our entire bank account. I had checked the account on Friday, and all our money was there. But on Monday, there was nothing. Because he used to spend a lot of time at the casino, I can only assume he gambled it away. I never found out what became of all our money.

Martin had a very small life insurance policy through our employer. It wasn't much, about $50,000, but it would be enough to enable me to keep the house, pay off bills, and hopefully keep me afloat so I would not have to file bankruptcy for a second time. That's the only hope I had of surviving this ordeal financially. But I did not get access to those funds for another four months because of an investigation that his family pushed.

Martin's family was convinced that he would never commit suicide. In their minds, this meant that I had to have either killed him, hired someone to kill him, that my mom had helped me kill him, or that I'd had an affair and had gotten that man to kill him. His family refused to believe what Martin had done, and his brother, who was a cop, pushed the police to investigate these allegations. Those few months were the worst in my entire life—and I had experienced a pretty shitty life up to this point! I had to rely on family and a couple of close friends for financial support just to feed my children and keep the lights on. I barely hung on mentally, financially, and physically. My rope was frayed and quickly unraveling.

After everything I had endured, those few months were the one period in my life during which I seriously contemplated suicide. I had my mom's Xanax in hand one night, while she was away for a couple hours, and I was ready to swallow the entire bottle. I was staying with her that night because my son and daughter were having their regularly allowed weekend visits with their other family, and I did not want to be alone. I was dealing with crippling fear that my attacker would return, even though, logically, I knew that was not possible. I think I also knew, deep inside, that I was close to being done with this life. And that scared me.

I was confounded by the lack of support I was receiving as the survivor of domestic violence. It was unfathomable to me that even though I was the one who had been attacked, I was being looked at like the whole nightmare was my fault. I felt like things would have been easier if I had just died that day. I had no money, and my daughter was completely traumatized. My son wasn't around when everything went down, but what happened affected him deeply as well. He just shut down on me and became distant. I felt like I didn't know how to be a mother anymore. I didn't know how I was going to recover from this nightmare or how I was going to be able to give my kids any semblance of a normal life. I just felt like I had nothing left to give. This world had managed to steal every ounce of light, every ounce of warmth, every ounce of fight, and every ounce of "give a shit" that I had left.

I was so close to ending my life that night that I actually had the pills in my mouth, ready to swallow . . . when in comes my guardian angel. I suddenly had images placed in my head of my daughter, who had just lost her father. I saw images of my son, who's dad had abandoned him. I realized that my children needed me and that I could not leave them both without any parent at all. I got that message loud and clear. My kids needed me.

I spit out all but a couple pills and opted for a nice long nap instead.

But that nap didn't fix everything. I was still facing so many challenges. Along with having the police digging into all aspects of my life, I was dealing with what to do about the funeral. I was dealing with the fact that I had no money and could not pay my bills. I was dealing with traumatized children, with my mother's trauma, and with my lawyer and this ridiculous investigation. I was dealing with so much that I never had time to grieve. I never had time to work through *my* pain and trauma. I never had time to process my experience as the victim.

Because I had no money, I had no choice but to go back to work just two short weeks after Martin attacked me and took his life. Two weeks! Fourteen days! I had to muster a tremendous amount of courage to face our friends, coworkers, boss, and everyone else at that company, knowing that this had now been moved to a full-blown investigation. Knowing that because people did not have the whole story, they just filled in the blanks themselves. Knowing that there would be those that blamed me. Not only that, but I was forced to go back to the very department that Martin and I had both worked in. I had to face the stares and the looks. I had to face the rumors that were now running rampant. I heard things like, Martin was shot, that he was stabbed multiple times, and that his death was "suspicious." I thought about quitting and starting over somewhere else, but my job was the only stability I had, and

I needed the paycheck.

I was so, so angry with Martin for leaving me with this mess. I was determined to not let him destroy my life from the grave. I was not going to let him win. I stayed put and I stood my ground. I just recently passed my twenty-three-year anniversary with the same company and am now a Senior Sales Operations Manager.

I fought back. I persevered. I never gave up.

SIXTEEN

My Father, the Funeral, and the Investigation

*"Kids have a hole in their soul in the shape of their dad.
And if a father is unwilling or unable to fill that hole,
it can leave a wound that is not easily healed."*
– Roland Warren

Five years before Martin killed himself, on my twenty-seventh birthday, I finally found my biological father. I think back to when I was a kid, and all the years I spent going through a five-inch-thick phone book, only to come up empty-handed. But once the internet became a thing, it was easy. My mom had provided me with enough information on my dad and his immediate family to get me started. Within just a few hours of searching the web, I found my father's brother. I called this uncle and left a message telling him who I was and that I was trying to find my dad. I left him all my contact information. That same day, my dad called me back.

I was so excited! All the fairy-tale stories I had imagined as a kid came rushing back to me. I began imaging that we would be super close, and that we would visit each other all the time. I felt my huge, gaping hole begin to fill. But like my childhood fantasies, these dreams were never realized.

At first, we corresponded on a regular basis, by phone and by email. I told him about my stepdad and how tough things were growing up, but I never got a straight answer as to why he chose to not help raise us. In my initial excitement, I bought a binder and printed out every single email he sent me. I did that for probably a year before growing weary of it. Then I began saving his emails in a folder on my computer. Over time, I stopped doing even that.

I went to visit my dad in California a couple times. The first time was with Martin and our daughter, when she was only about a year old. I really hoped my dad would visit me on a regular basis, since it was easier for one person to visit a family then for a family to visit one person. But he only came to visit me one time; just once. Don't get me wrong; I really, *really* appreciated that visit. I just wish he had come out more often. I invited him out to visit on every major holiday and in the summers. I had hoped he would get to know his grandchildren, but he never did.

In 2003, after my brutal attack and my husband's death by suicide, when it mattered the most, my dad showed up. I was thirty-two years old, and this was only the third time I had ever seen my father. He came out to help me when he learned of all that had happened. He also took out a loan from his 401k so that I could pay my bills and feed my kids. That was a godsend. He puttered around the house, fixing things that had been neglected, and just finding ways to help. He came out immediately and was able to attend the funeral with me. I did not want to go to the funeral as I was angry and still very traumatized. I only went because I thought others expected it from me. I did a lot of things back then because others expected it, but I did not do what I needed to do to take care of myself.

I also agreed to pay the funeral bill with the insurance money I had coming. I should never have agreed to this. I should never have had to pay for my attacker's funeral. I was trying to do the right thing and trying to appease his family. They asked that I pay for it; actually, they demanded it. I did not have much coming from insurance and could not afford the $10,000 it was going to cost, but I agreed to it anyway. I found myself trying to make everyone around me feel better, like somehow this was my fault and my mess to clean up.

I allowed Martin's family to make all the funeral arrangements. I let him be buried in their family cemetery. I wanted nothing to do with any of it. His family was hostile against me because they blamed me. One of his brothers even called me before the funeral and said, "I'm trying very hard not to come after you." I felt threatened; I felt like I was in danger. My cop friend and my dad both went to the funeral as protection. They kept an eye out to make sure no one did anything out of rage or emotion.

People did not understand why I was not going to the visitation that was scheduled the day before the funeral. It was an open casket visitation and there was absolutely no way I was going to subject myself to that. It was the only thing I found the strength to say "No" to. The thought of seeing my attacker's face threw me into a panic. Because people did not know the truth of what happened that day—they were not there, they did not go through it, and there was an ongoing investigation—they did not understand my actions. I was criticized for not wanting to be at the visitation and it fueled the rumors. I didn't care. Hell, I didn't even want to attend the funeral! I did it out of obligation. I was so sick from stress that I had lost weight, and I had no weight to lose at the time. I was already very lean, but when I bought a dress for the funeral, it was a size 3. I am five foot nine and I weighed maybe 120 pounds then. I was pale, thin, and exhausted. I was barely clinging to any sense of life. The therapist I was seeing to work through this latest trauma had me so heavily medicated that the funeral was a blur to me. Most days were a blur.

I did not have my daughter attend her father's funeral. She was only four years old and was taking medication prescribed by the therapist that she now needed to see to process her trauma and resolve her sleep issues. Instead of going to the funeral, she spent the day with a friend, but her older half-sister attended with her mother.

My father only stayed a short time and left soon after the funeral. I remember wishing that he would stay. I was scared, alone, lost, and could have used the support and the company. I even contemplated asking him if I could bring the kids to California and move in with him, but I had too much fear of starting over in a new place to even ask.

When my father left, I was terrified. I not only locked my children and myself in at night, but I kept a baseball bat and a can of wasp spray (I do not like guns) next to my bed. It was months before I could relax enough to not go to such extremes. It was months before I could sleep without weapons, or locked bedroom doors, or nightmares.

The Investigation

The investigation went on for months. I was afraid every single day during that time. Not because I was guilty of anything, but because I had watched too many television shows and heard too many stories of innocent people going to jail. I just knew that I would have to go to trial and defend myself for surviving that day. It was a level of stress I cannot even explain in words. The detectives assigned to the case interrogated my daughter, my mother, my coworkers, and anyone else they could think of. They confiscated my computer at work and dug through my life. The original death certificate was marked "unknown cause of death" until the investigation was complete, and the autopsy was finished. My entire life was put on hold while this was hanging over my head like a massive, suffocating, dark cloud. I could not move on, and I could not heal. I couldn't eat and I couldn't sleep. I could barely breathe. I only left the house to go to work.

I had to go to work every single day and find the courage to face my coworkers . . . Every. Single. Day. I learned to shut down my emotions and power through. I had already been isolated from most of my friends and even some of my family, and now I was isolating from everyone else around me as much as I could. I did not trust anyone, and I did not want to deal with either the accusatory stares or the sympathetic glances. I did my job and went home.

The only person I socialized with was my mom. But even then, I spent our time together trying to make her feel better because she was also traumatized by what had happened. I felt like her trauma was my fault because her home is where I chose to meet Martin that day. Fortunately, my brother worked at a building and lumber company that went in and restored her house when the police were done collecting evidence. They had to clean up the blood and replace carpet and flooring. Of course, this restoration project could not erase the memories for her; it had to have been almost impossible for her to stay there and relive them every day. My mother eventually moved, as did I. I could no longer be in the house where Martin and I had lived together. After dealing with all the fallout, I sold it as soon as I could, so I could try to start over in a fresh environment.

What really angered me about this whole ordeal was how adamant Martin's family was that everything was my fault. They refused to believe anything I said about his controlling behavior or that he took his own life; they refused to believe any of it! But what made me the angriest was when two key things came to light as a result of the investigation. It turns out that Martin had two instances of domestic violence linked to his first and second wives. This was information I was not privy to, and that neither he nor his family ever told me about. And yet, they refused to believe that he could be violent and that I might be telling the truth. The second thing I found out was that, after his first marriage fell apart, Martin checked himself into a hospital because he feared he would hurt himself. His family knew about this as well. And yet, they refused to believe he could be unstable or suicidal. I was furious that no one ever provided me with this information, and I was so angry that, knowing these things, his family was still trying to put the blame on me. I was angry that my life was being torn apart and it infuriated me to see that so few people believed me.

But my mom had my back. She believed me because she witnessed the horrors of that day. She knew the truth.

It also made me angry—and scared me—the day someone came to my door and served me with a legal document stating that I was a party involved in a murder investigation. I think it was a court order to have my daughter questioned, or for me to go back in and be questioned again. I'm not certain because all I could focus on was the "murder investigation" part of the document. I could not believe what I was seeing! Instantly, I felt physically ill. This was my worst fear all along. I immediately called my lawyer and he let loose on whomever created that court document. They said it was a mistake and that the document should not have stated such a thing. They (whoever "they" were) said they would correct it immediately, which they did. I felt like it was harassment; something done just to rattle me. That's how my life was for the few months this case was open.

At the end of the day, there was no case. There was no murder. There was no hitman involved or some seedy murder plot hatched by me and my mom. There were no prints on the knife except my late husband's. There was absolutely no evidence of anyone else being involved, and there was no evidence linking me to anything other than the truth I had been telling them all along. One police officer told me, "Well, we have never seen anything

like this before. People just don't commit suicide in this manner."
Apparently, because they had never seen it, it can't be true. Yes, it
was brutal. Yes, you don't hear about people killing themselves in
that manner. But a knife was the only weapon Martin had, and he
panicked. He was not in his right mind. It's not clean. It's not the
norm. But it happened.

After a few months, the autopsy report also came back, and
the coroner had indeed ruled it a suicide. After scouring his body,
evaluating the single wound, and confirming there were no defense wounds on him, the coroner communicated to the police
that there was no way I could have done this given the effort and
strength it would have taken, the angle of the point of entry, etc.
Nothing lined up with anything—except what I had been telling
them all along.

There are no words to express the relief I felt when the case
was officially closed and the final death certificate was released.
The stress of it all was so debilitating that I cried for hours when
my lawyer told me it was over. The pressure of trying to work
and trying to take care of my children, by myself, had been overwhelming. I was totally and utterly spent.

After the case was closed, I had one coworker come up to me
and say, "I guess you got away with murder." I consider myself
to be very professional at work and I do everything I can to keep
my personal life apart from my work life. I strive to behave in a
manner that is respectful and HR-appropriate. But in that moment,
I could not hold my tongue. In that moment, I lashed out at her
with, "Fuck you!"

I had had enough of feeling like everything was my fault. I

had had enough of the stares and the rumors. I had had enough of feeling like I should not be at work. I had had enough of Martin's crazy family and the threats. Even after all the evidence came in and the case was closed, the family still—to this day!—refuses to believe any of it. They often tell my daughter that one day they will tell her the truth, and that she needs to know the truth. Really?! The truth? She was there! She knows the truth because she lived it.

As I previously mentioned, during our marriage, Martin and I obtained custody of his first daughter, who was a pre-teen when she came to live with us. Her mom agreed to sign her over to us because she knew we had too much incriminating evidence on her to fight us and because she could not provide a safe and healthy environment for her daughter. The irony of the fact that our home was healthier than hers has never been lost on me! I have nothing bad to say about Martin's abilities as a father or how much he loved his girls. I know he was arrested in the past for being delinquent on child support, but he was striving to turn things around and wanted to do better for his first daughter.

Around midnight on the same night that her father passed, the mom of Martin's first daughter showed up at my door to reclaim her. I had no grounds to fight this because she was not my child. I had no choice but to let her mom take her. Besides, after the horrific events of that day, I was in no place mentally to put up any kind of fight. I packed up as much of her stuff as I could, and she left that night with her mom, never to return. That meant that my daughter lost her father and her half-sister, all in one day.

The guilt I felt over my daughter's losses was overwhelming.

That's why, in the midst of everything else I was dealing with, I also took responsibility for trying to clean up this new mess with Martin's first daughter. When I eventually received the money from the insurance company, along with spending over $10,000 on the funeral of my attacker, I spent over $5,000 on his daughter's lawyer fees. I should never have done these things, but I was not strong enough to understand that I needed to take care of myself and my children first and foremost. Instead, I thought it was my place to make sure Martin's oldest daughter was taken care of, and I knew that meant not being with her mom. That's why I paid to help her aunt gain custody of her over her mother. But it wasn't my place. That was that family's mess to deal with, while I should have been focusing on climbing out of the financial hole in which Martin had left me and my children.

The situation with his first daughter ended up being a fiasco and, once I paid for the attorney, I bowed out of it. At one point, the mother took off with her and I think she stayed with her for quite some time. I am relieved to know that Martin's oldest daughter grew up to be a wonderful person. She has reconnected with her half-sister (my daughter), and is now happy and in a healthy relationship of her own. It does my heart good to know that she managed to work her way through the loss of her father, and the mess that was her childhood, and that she was strong enough to persevere.

SEVENTEEN

Alcoholic #2 Becomes Husband #3

"The narcissist blames his/her behavior on something that you are or aren't doing."

–Melanie Tonia Evans

My Daughter the Matchmaker

After Martin killed himself and his oldest daughter was taken away by her mother, I became a single mom with two children. I was only thirty-five, so it's not like I was an old maid, but for some reason, my daughter became very concerned about me being alone. She was only four when she lost her father, but she understood he was not coming back. From then on, she kept her eyes out for prospects and frequently told me, "Mom, you need a honey."

I assured her multiple times that "Mom is just fine on her own" and that I did not need a honey. I wanted her to grow up strong and independent and to not feel like she had to have a man to complete her. I figured this was as good a time as any to begin instilling these ideas! Despite my protests, she kept pushing, and I kept pushing back. My daughter was an unbelievably stubborn child, but she always had a very caring nature.

She was so persistent that, one day, when my daughter saw a homeless man, she excitedly piped up from the back seat, "Mommy, that man needs a place to live, and you need a honey!" I found her four-year-old logic to be quite impressive! Through my giggles I responded, "Sweetie, let's raise our standards just a bit. I think we can do better." Undeterred, my daughter continued to try and set me up.

I tried going on a date here and there, but honestly, my heart was not in it. I was still traumatized from what had recently happened with Martin. I was still carrying the weight of the guilt, shame, bad decisions, and horrific events from my entire past. This weight was now so heavy that I was embarrassed to even try and connect with people anymore. If I connected with people, they would eventually ask me questions about myself, and I had no interest in answering any questions about my life. I shoved everything down, like I had learned to do as a child. I pretended I was fine. I pretended I did not need anyone because it was easier than admitting what I really thought: that I would be alone the rest of my life. After all, what man would be willing to take on this train wreck? And technically, I did not need anyone. I had a good job and could afford to take care of my children. Granted, I was barely making ends meet, but the bills were getting paid. Somehow, I was still surviving.

One day, as I was picking up my daughter from daycare, a much younger man told me he was one of her teachers. "Your daughter asked me to ask you out on a date, so that's what I'm doing. Would you like to go out with me?" Of course, I was mortified and apologized profusely. I also accepted his invitation. He was cute and sweet and great with kids, so I thought, "Why not?"

I spent the entire drive home trying to explain to my daughter, as gently as I could, that she could not go around asking men to take me out. I told her that when I was ready, I would choose someone to date. I don't think anything I said made an impression on her because she just sat in her booster seat and beamed. She was obviously very proud of herself for finding mommy a honey.

After that first date, Mike and I started seeing each other regularly. He soon became a permanent fixture in our lives.

There were so many red flags, right from the beginning. Mike was all over the place regarding his career. He ultimately wanted to be a teacher but made little effort to get there. Much of his life was in disarray. He consistently overdrew his checking account. Either he did not understand how to balance a checkbook or he was too consumed with drinking and playing video games to manage common daily tasks. Mike did not pay his utility bills on time, so something was always getting disconnected. He operated more like a teenager than a twenty-five-year-old man. I chalked all this up to him still being young—eight years younger than me—and told myself he would mature over time. I convinced myself that this was normal for people his age. Because I had been out on my own since I was seventeen, I'd had to grow up quickly, so surely that is why I was more responsible. Plus, Mike had no children, and I had two, so of course I was going to act more responsibly.

Ignoring all the red flags, I continued to date Mike, not out of love or adoration, but because I honestly did not think I had any other options. Besides that, I was completely exhausted. Despite what I told my daughter, I had finally reached the point in my life where I did not think I could do it on my own any longer. The past had taken its toll on me and, in my mind, I needed someone to carry the burden for a while.

I know it was completely unfair of me to expect that from anyone, but the latest horrible events and the ever-present weight of my past had robbed me of what little energy I had left. After dating for a year, Mike proposed and I said, "Yes," with no previous discussion of marriage. We eloped and got married at the courthouse. That was fine with me since, in my mind, it was not a celebration . . . it was a concession.

Mike insisted that he have two sons; that was non-negotiable. I already had two children, and my body was tired. I was tired. But I felt like I needed to comply with his wishes to be a good wife; to keep him happy. The first pregnancy occurred around the same time we married, but it ended in a miscarriage. I honestly believe that loss was stress induced. At Mike's direction, I became pregnant again almost immediately after the miscarriage. His dream was to have two boys, close in age, so just months after giving birth, I became pregnant one last time with his second son and my fourth child.

Down That Road Again

As with most abusers, Mike was very charming at first. But

certain things fueled his insecurities. As he became increasingly jealous, I began to feel that old familiar stress and anxiety. I feared I was starting down that same old road to marital unhappiness.

When I transferred to the sales department at work to position myself for better opportunities, Mike did not like that most of the employees in the department were men. He also did not like that this new position required me to travel with my male colleagues. When I had to go to China for a business trip, he actually went through my suitcase and pulled out anything he felt was "not acceptable" to wear on the trip. He would get upset at me for putting on makeup and doing my hair for work. He did not want me dressing up but insisted that I should wear sweats . . . in a business office! One night we were at a department Christmas dinner and he behaved like a total ass. I was so embarrassed that I never took him around my coworkers again.

When my boss told me I did not need a bachelor degree to get promoted to management, but I did have to be working towards it, I started taking one online college course each semester. I was fortunate that my workplace offered a nice tuition reimbursement program. That, along with the flexibility of online classes, made it feasible for me to do this, even with four children. Mike did not like how much time my class took in the evenings. "You're neglecting me," he'd say. It drove him nuts that my attention was diverted elsewhere. One evening, he almost broke my laptop as he tried to grab it away from me so I couldn't do my homework.

Mike was so codependent (although I didn't even know this term then) that it made it very difficult for me to be my own person in the marriage. If he was upset, he wanted me to be upset. If he was happy, I needed to be happy. If he was bummed out and I was in a good mood then "I was a horrible wife who didn't support him." It was exhausting.

Another source of contention was the fact that I was trying to get back into shape after having back-to-back pregnancies. Since Mike would not help with the babies so I could go to a gym, I bought a treadmill. The day he came home and found it set up in the living room, he was angry. Mike would make fun of me while I was running on it. He became upset when I worked out, accusing me of doing it "for all the men at work."

These absurdities were only part of the problem I had with the marriage. Mike's intense mood swings and depression, the verbal abuse, and his addiction to pain medication, muscle relaxers, and alcohol were the bigger issues. He would attempt to hide his alcohol and deny he was drinking. He would deny he was taking medication; he would deny having any addiction issues at all. When I had a C-section with my last son, Mike would steal my pain medication. When I confronted him, he blamed my teenage son and told me he was the one taking my medication. I knew for a fact that this was a lie because my son had severe allergies to pain meds so he steered clear of prescription pain medication.

When I would find Mike's alcohol hidden in the garage, he would blame me for his drinking. "If you and my mom would just get along, I wouldn't have to drink." He would also blame me for his other problems. "If you would not wear make-up and not dress up when you go to work, I would trust you more. I wouldn't be so jealous." "If you would just love me enough, I wouldn't get so depressed." The blame game was one of his favorites.

It's no surprise that Mike had trouble keeping a job. He would either quit or get fired, and he could never stay focused on what he wanted to do for a career. He took additional classes so he could get a teaching job in Arkansas with his History degree. Actually, the truth is that I took the classes for him so that he would pass the course. Mike had trouble finding an open position, so he opted to work part-time as a substitute teacher, hoping this would lead to a full-time position. It never did, and this move buried us financially. Now Mike was not only getting a pay cut, but he was just working part-time. I always made more than him, but now that gap was even greater.

I tried to be the dutiful wife and support his dreams. After all, I had always wanted someone to support my dreams, so I felt it would be hypocritical of me not to support his. But I finally had to have a difficult discussion with Mike and tell him that we could not survive financially if he did not get a full-time job. We were out of money, and we were out of options. His job search was a long, drawn-out, drama-filled process that finally resulted in him getting a job at Walmart. His brother, who worked there, got him an interview. Mike did not go to the interview willingly, and he did not go to work without reminding me daily that I was a horrible wife for making him get a different job.

Life with Mike was an extreme roller coaster ride, and I wanted off in the worst way. But I stayed because he would threaten to kill himself if I left. Mentally and emotionally, I just could not go through that again. One time, Mike locked himself in the bathroom and wrote out a list of the pros and cons of killing himself. I still have that list. I kept it just in case I ever got up the courage to go through with a divorce. But I didn't muster that courage for several more years. I couldn't bear the thought of having two husbands die by suicide, especially after all I had endured with Martin's investigation. I stayed with Mike out of fear and self-preservation—and I was miserable.

My Third Turning Point: Protecting My Children

In the past, my abusers had always focused their physical and verbal abuse on me, so I felt like my children were protected. Since my kids were never physically harmed, in my mind, I was shielding them. Even my daughter was completely unaware of her father's controlling behavior. Martin adored her, and he was a great dad. Likewise, Mike would never have said or done anything to hurt his boys or my son and daughter. He loved them tremendously.

That's why he made every attempt to hide his outbursts and meltdowns, his depression and his verbal attacks from them. But what neither of us realized was that, even though our little boys may not have seen anything, they could hear him. And they were now old enough to understand the abusive things their father was saying to their mother. Late at night, after they went to bed, my toddlers could hear their father's words, and those words weighed on them.

The first time I became aware of this was when our boys were two- and three- years old. Mike and I had been up much of the night, fighting about something. That night, the fight was especially volatile, with Mike delivering the same repeated verbal assaults. It was always a version of, "You're a horrible mom and the kids hate you," and, "No wonder your last husband killed himself. It's your fault because you're a bad wife." Sometimes, just for effect, he would throw in, "I'm going to kill myself, so you have to live with that too."

Mike's tactics were predictable, but that night he veered from his standard assault and ramped it up a notch. He grabbed the butcher knife out of its block and threatened me with it. Since being held hostage at knife point by my previous husband, I was terrified of knives; I had extreme anxiety over just having them in the house. The PTSD I experienced would throw me into a physical state of panic. In the past, I had begged Mike to get rid of that particular knife, but I think he enjoyed keeping it because he knew how much it upset me. For him to threaten me that night with that particular knife was a new low, even for him.

The next morning, when my three-year-old came out of his room, he was crying. Kneeling beside him I asked, "Why are you crying?" I will never forget what happened next. Through teary eyes he looked at me and said, "I don't think you're a bad mom. I love you."

My heart shattered. It literally broke into a thousand pieces.

That was the moment I decided I was not going to put them through what I grew up with. I was going to do things differently. I was going to do better and I was going to break the cycle of violence and abuse. I decided at that moment that I was done—and the divorce quickly followed. There was no suicide attempt, there was little drama, and I maintained custody of the boys. For those five miserable years that we were married, Mike had just been full of hot air. I regretted letting his threats and my fears get the best of me. I regretted not making that decision sooner.

PART FIVE

MY FORTIES: HEALING BEGINS

EIGHTEEN

My Biggest Fan

*"One of the hardest things was learning
that I was worth recovery."*
Demi Lovato

When I divorced my third husband, my life improved considerably. Yes, it was stressful being the single mom of four children, but I was happy because there was no one there to tell me what to do, to control me, abuse me, isolate me, or tell me that I was not enough. I finally found peace being by myself. I even enjoyed my own company. I also enjoyed the routine I had developed and the safe place I had created for my children. I made a quiet promise to myself that there would never be any type of violence or abuse in my house again.

At first, I made this promise solely for my children. They deserved better. Over time, I realized that I, too, deserved better. Somehow, somewhere, there was still something left inside me that drove me to believe that I was worth more—even after four decades of being told otherwise. There was just enough spark smoldering inside for me to keep up the fight. My abusers did not win. My guardian angel did not spend all those years chasing me around, pulling me out of death's grasp, just for me to give up when the coast was finally clear. I believe she would have been disappointed if I had decided to throw in the towel and shut out the world, especially now that I had a real chance to figure out what I wanted from life and who I wanted to be.

Part of my drive to do better, to make better decisions, and to be better came from my realization that maybe I was here for a reason. It just didn't make sense to think that I had gone through everything I had experienced—all that suffering—for absolutely no reason. This realization did not dawn on me in a sudden "Aha!" moment. Instead, it grew slowly. Being on my own with my children and free from the drama of my past relationships gave me just enough space to look back over my life. This prompted me to start questioning the journey I was on. The thought that maybe my life had a purpose inspired me to dig in my heels and get serious about fixing my head, repairing my heart, and creating a better life.

Dating Differently in My Forties

As part of my self-improvement journey, I wanted to experience a healthy relationship. Now that I was content to be on my own, I knew I wouldn't be dating for the wrong reason—just so I wouldn't be alone. I started trusting myself to make better decisions. I had no desire to marry again, but I did want to know what "normal" looked like. I just wanted to be with someone who was nice to me. I wanted to experience a relationship where I could still be an independent person while also being connected to someone.

I did not know how to find such a relationship, but I've learned that the first step to any growth is being willing to change, being willing to do the work it takes to heal.

By 2010, dating apps were becoming popular. This seemed like a great option for me, seeing as I was too old for the bar scene and way too busy to spend lots of time trying to find ways to meet people. It doesn't get any easier than scrolling through a catalogue of options and reading all about potential candidates! I could even set a filter and weed out some of what I knew for a fact that I did not want.

I loved that filter option because I knew for sure that there were some things that were deal-breakers. I had absolutely no interest in a man much younger or much older than myself. My last husband was eight years younger than me, and it was like babysitting. Gerald had been ten years older, and that hadn't worked either. The ideal candidate must have a career and make at least as much as myself—preferably more. With Mike, I had been down the road where I was the bread winner, and I was not going there again.

Religion was a touchy subject because I could not be with someone that was super religious. After my negative childhood experiences with religion, I had not stepped foot in a church since I left home as a teenager, and I had no plans to do so again. But I did want to find someone who shared views similar to mine—someone who was very spiritual, who believed in a higher power, and who perhaps even shared my belief in spirits and angels. Since I live in the Bible Belt of Arkansas, I realized these criteria could be highly problematic. Everyone goes to church here and everyone just assumes that everyone else goes to church. In fact, I am always surprised by the looks I used to get (and still get today) when I mention that I don't go to church. You would think I had just admitted to being a serial killer!

Having children was not an initial "must have," but after dating a couple men that did not have kids, it became one. Those men did not understand the time constraints I had or that I could not just drop what I was doing on a whim and go on a date or out of town for the weekend. It became apparent that, to date successfully, it was best to date a man who was in the same situation, who understood that the kids always came first.

Unfortunately, when I set all these parameters, it drained most of the water from the dating pool! It's a good thing I was not in a hurry or did not feel like I had to date to be happy. This time, I was not dating to escape my stepdad or because I could not afford to take care of my myself and my kids. I was not dating because I could not be alone or because I felt too exhausted to make a go of it on my own. This time, I could wait patiently until I found someone worthy of my time. It took a few rounds for me to find my best friend, my soul mate, my biggest fan. I guess I had to pay my dating dues first.

The first man I found through the dating app was so controlling of his environment that it triggered my PTSD. He reminded me of Martin, so I did not date him long. His house was spotless, with not a thing out of place. One time I bumped into his couch and he came over and fanatically lined it back up to where it "belonged." The next date he was making drinks for us and asked me to fold the napkins in quarters so he could place the drinks on them. After I had incorrectly folded the napkins, he was kind enough to correct me and then re-explain and re-fold the napkins. I mean, thank goodness! That could have been a napkin disaster! The last straw for me was when he mentioned something about kids and how loud and messy they were. Done. Next.

I went out a few times with a man who had an amazing job and made quite a bit of money. He had custody of his children and a live-in nanny. He was even into fitness! That was great, because I was just getting back into running and thought a fitness buddy would be a nice bonus. Initially, I thought it was going to be a perfect match.

On our second date, he had to leave early because his ex-wife was staying with him and she was demanding he come home. She was highly suicidal, and he was always worried about her, so she stayed with him quite a bit. I sensed right off the bat that this was not a healthy dynamic. I also discovered that his live-in nanny was a college girl that he thought was attractive and that they sat around and drank together . . . often.

Nope. I did not need any of this in my life. This was not the healthy relationship I was seeking. The situation with his nanny gave me immediate flashbacks to Gerald and his Hooter girls. And whether this man's relationship with his nanny was innocent or not, I was not even willing to go down that road to find out. My abusers had taught me many lessons, and I was now hyper-sensitive to any red flags, even potential ones. My past experiences had also trained my senses to react to negative situations or negative traits in someone—the hair would literally stand up on the back of my neck. That's when I knew I needed to pay attention. Because I was having this physical reaction and seeing red flags in this situation, I trusted my intuition and moved on.

Another man I dated was a very nice person with a good job, but he seemed distracted on our first two dates. After the second date, he called me to apologize for being distant and explained that he had not felt good for a while. He was having sinus issues and was going to a doctor that week. He said he'd call me after that, and we'd go out when he was feeling better. But he never called. Because I never heard from him and had never really felt any sparks there, I didn't reach out. About a year later, I learned from a mutual acquaintance that this man, who was only in his forties, had died. His sinus infection ended up being an advanced-stage, malignant tumor, which is why I never heard from him again. Although I had only been on two dates with him, the news of his death rattled me.

James

I found my soul mate, my best friend, and my biggest fan in the next man I dated. In my mind, this was another "God deal" because I had passed up James' picture and profile many times. I passed it up because the photo he chose as his cover shot showed him at a bar with friends. By this point in my life, I'd had my fill of drinking and I was not going to date someone that was still going to bars. I just couldn't do it anymore. It's not that I expected my dates to totally abstain from alcohol; I just needed someone who rarely drank. James later told me that he was just days away from letting his membership on that dating app expire. He had been having the same poor results I was experiencing. The only reason we met is because I decided to look beyond the cover photos of the men that showed up in my filter and go into their profiles to read about them. I wanted to see other pictures. I wanted to learn more about their hobbies and try to understand who they were. By judging someone on the basis of just one photo, I realized I might miss out on someone great. And I was right. I almost did!

When I opened his profile, I noticed James had sent me a message a couple of weeks earlier. I read his profile… and it was surprisingly similar to mine. James listed out what he wanted and what he didn't want. I had set up my profile in the same manner. He had three children, ages seven, ten, and fourteen, who stayed with him every other weekend and during the summers. James also noted that he did not drink, which was a huge bonus to me, as long as it was not because he was super religious. I held my breath on that one and made a mental note to learn more about this if we ended up going on a date. I then came across a photo of him and his daughter. His blue eyes and soul-piercing smile were what got me.

Because of that picture, I responded to his message. James wrote back that very day and we began chatting over instant messaging. We bantered back and forth for a couple of hours, both trying to outwit the other. He made me laugh and that was very, very important. At that time, I did not have much laughter in my life, and I wanted to change that.

I had an opening to inquire about the "do not drink" on his profile, so I asked him if that was due to religious beliefs. He responded that he was not overly religious, but he didn't drink because "His life just worked better for him when he didn't." That was code for "I'm an alcoholic," but I didn't know that because, back then, I did not understand what an alcoholic was. I also didn't realize that I had already dated one and married and divorced another. Because I didn't catch James' drift, I proceeded to embarrass myself by making a joke about being in a twelve-step program. I didn't even really know what that was, but I was trying to be witty and funny and catch his attention. I must have made some sort of an impression because James asked me out to coffee, then changed it to a dinner date.

The night of our date, it was pouring rain. James was kind enough to choose a location closer to me so I did not have to drive as far in the weather. That's just how he operates. He is very caring and chivalrous, still, to this day. I was relieved when I saw him at the restaurant, in jeans and a sports coat, looking so handsome. I was relieved because sometimes when you meet someone for a date, they look nothing like their profile picture. But James had a nice head of thick hair, striking blue eyes, and a smile that melted my guarded heart.

Conversation came easy to us, but I still ordered a margarita to ease my nerves. I was not a big drinker, but I did like an occasional margarita with Mexican food. James did not order any alcohol and I remember thinking that he was being honest about not drinking. Somewhere in the middle of dinner, he confessed to me that he was a recovering alcoholic and that he attended a twelve-step program. I was horrified, seeing as I had made a joke about that earlier. I was embarrassed and apologized for making such an insensitive remark, but he took it all in stride.

Considering my past experiences with men who drank too much, you would think that would have been the end of that date and that potential relationship. In fact, as he continued to tell me about his life, I should have just excused myself from the meal and left—not just walked out of the restaurant, but run as fast as I could. I was looking for normal and healthy, remember? This had all the makings of being the opposite of that.

Along with being a recovering alcoholic, James shared that he was separated and in the process of getting a divorce. He had been married three times—twice to the same woman. Despite these things, I was drawn in and intrigued by his brutal honesty. I was shocked at how vulnerable he was willing to be. I had never witnessed that kind of transparency. It both surprised and bewildered me—and it also hooked me. I had not experienced such honesty from a man before, or from anyone, for that manner. That is why I stayed and finished dinner and why I continued to date him. He was honest, sensitive, vulnerable, handsome, and he had a good job. It was too good to be true. I spent the next few months waiting for the other shoe to drop. I had one foot in the trust circle and one foot out, ready to run.

Since I had already tried marriage three times with no success, I had no interest in remarrying. James was also done with marriage because he, too, had been married three times. I'm not sure if there was a defining moment for him when he realized he was open to giving it another shot, but there was for me. After a few months of dating, there was one incident that let me know I was going to marry this man.

James traveled frequently for his job. On this particular evening, he had just returned from a business trip, looking all handsome in his suit and tie. We had already made plans to take my younger boys to see Christmas lights on the local square, so we loaded my then three- and four-year-old into their booster seats and headed out. One of my sons has an incredibly sensitive stomach (still to this day) and gets car sick easily. After winding through neighborhoods to look at more lights, he threw up all over himself in the back seat of my suburban. Without giving it a second thought, James drove to a car wash, took off his suit jacket, and with his dress shirt and tie still on, climbed into the back seat with a car wash vacuum hose and cleaned up my son and his surroundings.

That's probably not the romantic moment most women dream about, but for me, that was it. I told myself, "I'm going to marry this man," and I did. We married in 2011, about a year after we started dating. We've been together thirteen years now, and it's been wonderful. James builds me up, supports my dreams, and reinforces my self-worth and confidence. And . . . he introduced me to steps I could take towards healing and recovery.

NINETEEN

First Steps to Healing

"I'm not telling you it's going to be easy,
I'm telling you it's going to be worth it."

--Anonymous

During the time James and I were dating, I took some important first steps on the journey of healing my body image. As I have already shared, my childhood monster, Norman, inflicted deep psychological wounds on my body image. To this day, I still battle the negative messaging that he programmed into me and that Gerald reinforced by body shaming me. I am more capable of managing this negative messaging now, with the work I have done, but I know the emotional scars will never completely disappear. I don't foresee myself ever not worrying about weight gain, or not being hyper conscious about what I eat, or how many calories I consume a day.

I'll never forget the incident that first made James aware of the depths of my body image struggles. One night, I was at my house and tripped and fell against a large bed post, splitting my head open like a watermelon. I started to black out, but managed to call my mom, who came and rushed me to the hospital. The gash required thirteen stitches on my forehead. My forehead! Right where everyone could see them! I would not be able to hide this scar like I hid the huge scar from my kidney surgery and the tummy-length scar from my car accident. Having a visible scar was my worst body image nightmare.

Understanding my scar-related anxiety, Mom would not allow an ER doctor to stitch me up. Instead, she insisted that someone with experience in cosmetic surgery do the job. I am so glad she was there to be my advocate, because now, that scar over my eye is no longer visible. But I didn't know then that this would be the outcome.

When I told James what happened, and about the possible scar on my forehead, my deeply engrained fears of ridicule and rejection were so strong that I broke down in tears. I was so afraid he would break up with me! I know how irrational this sounds now, but back then, that is how messed up I was regarding body image. James was taken aback to know that I could even imagine that he might end our relationship over a scar.

Tattoos

I was so grateful to know that James did not care about my scars. And I was thrilled to discover that he loved tattoos! After my grandparents' negative reaction, I was relieved that he did not judge or make me feel "less than" because of the two small tattoos I already had. I was so excited to share the love of ink with the man I was dating! Once James learned of the shame I felt because of my scars, he suggested that I get tattoos to cover them. I had not even known that scars could be tattooed over, but I loved the idea.

Of the several tattoos I have gotten since being with James, my two favorites are the ones that now cover up both of my surgical scars. The first one had to be large enough to run around the entire left side of my body and up part of my back, because that's how large the scar was from my kidney operation. I found a drawing of a guardian angel kneeling, crouched over, looking exhausted. I knew instantly that this was the design I wanted. Since my guardian angel had been doing the hard work of keeping me alive and out of trouble for years, I knew she must look just like this. The wings of the design were large enough to extend across my entire side and cover every bit of my scar. I was not prepared for how much it hurt getting inked in that area, but I powered through. This particular tattoo is now my favorite. It is more than just a design to cover up a scar that had negatively impacted my body image since I was five years old; it is a tribute to my guardian angel that has kept me alive all these years.

It was a bit trickier finding a design to cover the scar on my stomach that ran all the way from my belly button to just underneath the middle of my breasts. I finally let the tattoo artist design something. He came up with a flower that fit nicely over the scar. I was very happy with how it turned out, but again, was not prepared for how much it hurt to get inked on my tummy. It was worse than having my side done. But the results were well worth the pain because they enabled me to wear my first bikini at the age of forty.

While wearing a bikini may not seem like a big deal to some people, for me, it represented just how many steps I had taken towards healing my body image. I used to have extreme anxiety going out in public in a one-piece swimsuit. In fact, I could not even go to the neighborhood pool by myself because I would have an anxiety attack. Even with my new tattoos covering the two scars that had tormented me for so much of my life, it still wasn't easy for me to wear a bikini in public. Just because my scars were now magically invisible, my body image issues were so deep-seated that it still took time, and much encouragement from James, for me to feel somewhat comfortable in a two-piece swimsuit. But having powered through the physical pain of getting my tattoos, I knew I could power through this psychological discomfort as well. Because Norman had made me feel like a freak because of my scars, and Gerald had called me "Frankenstein," I saw wearing a bikini as a concrete action I could take to remove those broken bricks of negative messaging from the shaky foundation of my low self-esteem. Wearing a bikini was a way to replace those faulty bricks with strong, solid bricks that built up my self-worth. It was a way of proving to myself that my abusers hadn't won and that I could still heal my life.

Every day I am grateful to James for loving me, scars and all, and for giving me the idea to tattoo over my scars, and for encouraging me to wear a bikini. And every day I am grateful to God that, just when I was at a point where I wanted to heal but did not yet know how to do so, He brought James into my life.

Twelve Step Programs

When James and I met, I knew nothing about alcoholism, twelve-step programs, or recovery. I thought these programs were short-term regimens that one would go through, complete the steps, and then be cured. It wasn't until I started dating a recovering alcoholic that I began to understand what it was really all about.

James had been in and out of recovery since his twenties and in and out of sobriety since his twenties, as well. I was shocked when I discovered that he still went to multiple meetings a week. He was newly sober, again, and aggressively working the steps, again. I thought, "Okay. He needs to go through the program again, because he had a slip. But when he's done, that will be the end of that." Wrong!

When I finally began to understand that recovery and attending meetings are a way of life for James, I asked him if I could attend one of the open meetings to get a better understanding of the disease. He told me that my wanting to get to know him at that level meant a great deal to him.

Little did I know that attending this meeting would mean a great deal to me, too. Even though I am not an alcoholic, attending those open meetings became a significant step on my path to healing. They are where I first learned about the alcoholics in my past. Most importantly, I learned that I wasn't the reason they behaved the way they did; it was the drinking, it was their demons, it was the disease. This new insight allowed me to replace a whole section of broken bricks with strong, positive messaging. This new understanding helped me rebuild my self-esteem.

This Twelve Step Program was also where I learned the term "codependency" and what it is. Codependency is a way of behaving in relationships where you persistently prioritize someone else's desires or happiness over your own, something I had continually done in all my previous relationships. Another characteristic of codependency is allowing your mood to be determined by how someone else is feeling or behaving. I immediately understood this concept, because that was what Mike had done. Once I thought more deeply about this aspect of codependency, I realized I had also allowed my moods and my happiness to be impacted by the feelings and behaviors of the men I dated or married. I also learned that codependent behavior is usually motivated by fears of rejection and low self-esteem, and that was certainly true in my case.

Learning about alcoholism and codependency allowed me to go back and review my life through a different lens. In the past, I had always viewed the horrible things I had experienced as things that had happened because I was no good, or I was faulty. And because I thought that I was the problem, a part of me also believed that I deserved all the pain and suffering I experienced. But understanding the disease of alcoholism and the dynamics of codependency helped me understand why I operated the way I did in certain relationships. It gave me insights into the part I played in creating and enabling those unhealthy relationships. Understanding my part in the process was a necessary step to stopping the cycle of me ending up in abusive relationships. Once I realized the part I was playing, I started moving from being a helpless victim to being someone who had the power and the ability to create a better life for myself and for my children.

I started attending these open Twelve Step meetings on a regular basis, not only to support James, but for me too. At first, I was petrified. I was still suffering from debilitating anxiety whenever I went somewhere new or when I had to be around new people. It was a very long time before I stopped feeling anxious, but I kept showing up. The people in the program were some of the warmest individuals I had ever met. They made me feel safe and accepted.

Along with becoming educated about the disease of alcoholism and the dynamics of codependency, I learned tools that began to help me with my everyday life. Sayings like "One day at a time" and "Let go and let God" became part of my daily coping mechanisms. In the past, the only way I had known to cope was to shut off my emotions, bury them deep down inside, and build a very large wall around myself. But being around these warm, supportive people in the program made we want to operate differently. I wanted to be able to connect with people again. I wanted to do better.

Once I realized that I was not just a helpless victim, once I began to see that my life had potential, I could not go back to just shoving everything down and pretending like it didn't matter. I could not go back to being a robot or just getting through the days with no joy. My defense mechanisms were as broken as I was; they were not serving me as they did in the past. I couldn't go back. I had to move forward. The open Twelve Step meetings that James and I attended regularly helped me do that. It still took a few years for me to get so desperate that I was willing to take the life changing step of attending Hoffman, but I know I would never have gone there if I had not already experienced my first steps to recovery within the four walls of those twelve-step rooms.

TWENTY

Hoffman

"Your trauma is not your fault,
but your healing is your responsibility."

@elizabethwirija

Soon after we married, James began encouraging me to go to a program called Hoffman. Hoffman is a residential week of intense group and individual sharing and therapy that incorporates experiential activities into the healing process. It promised to help me change the negative programming I had received as a child, break the unhealthy patterns I'd been engaging in, and give me tools to rewire my brain. It sounded intriguing to me and awful—all at the same time! My anxiety over the thought of spending a week baring my soul to strangers was crippling. But the weight of the guilt, shame, pain, and heaviness of the past forty years finally became even more crippling.

My Oldest Son

One additional development adding to the heaviness I already carried was the rift that had developed between me and my oldest son. Around the time I married James, my son turned eighteen and his father came back into his life. From the time I won custody of my son when he was six, Peter never exercised his visitation rights, and I cannot count the number of times I had to take him to court for child support arrearages. Then, for a couple of years I could not even find him to take him to court. Then one day my sister-in-law called. She told me Peter had been pulled over and the police found lots of meth and over $20,000 in his vehicle. He ended up in jail for over two years due to the drug charges. At the hearing, the judge told Peter he was not allowed to see his son until he finished serving his sentence and could prove he was cleaned up and free from drugs.

When he got out of jail, my son's father did eventually clean up his life. When he came back into my son's life and built a relationship with him, I was glad to see it. But then my ex began filling his head with untruths, implying I was the reason Peter was not around when he was a kid. Contrary to what my son came to believe, I was not the one that kept him away from his father. It was Peter's decisions that led to that. I did put him in jail from time to time over child support, but he was never there for more than a few days. Peter's mother would always show up with the money to bail him out.

My son not only built a relationship with his father, but he also maintained his relationship with Mike, who had been his second stepdad. Mike relished painting me as the bad parent. And I will admit, there were ways that I had let my son down as a parent—never intentionally—but nevertheless. The influence of both of these men, and the impact of my actions, despite my best intentions, soon led to my son having nothing to do with me. This broke my heart.

Buried Emotions

The growing heaviness of all the pain I was carrying brought me to the point where I was desperate enough to give Hoffman a try. The day I finally made the decision to go I was in the shower and had one of the emotional breakdowns I endured from time to time. Crying hysterically and shaking uncontrollably, I was unable to catch my breath. These episodes never lasted long, but they were intense. I think these little breakdowns were a pressure release valve that allowed the years of emotions I had buried deep down inside me to escape in a way that kept me from exploding—or imploding.

I had gotten very good at burying my feelings. In fact, I was more like a robot than a warm, feeling being around everyone except my children. That defense mechanism allowed me to survive my past, but it was not serving me well in the present. The problem was that these breakdowns were getting worse as I became more aware of how I shoved everything down and pretended like nothing had happened. The more time I spent in the rooms of recovery with my husband, the more I began to understand just how broken my mind was and just how badly I wanted to actually feel something, to change, to love myself, and to find relief.

Once I became desperate enough to try Hoffman, James and I scraped together the $5,000 that it cost to attend the one located in Napa Valley, California. Then I had to sit down, write out my story, and answer so many uncomfortable questions. It was the first time I put any of it to paper. Up to this point, I had only told my full story to James. Of course, my mom knew, because she had been there with me through it all. Other than that, no one else was aware of the dark places my life had taken me and of all I had endured. Now, if I wanted to heal, I was going to have to be honest and transparent when submitting my documents to Hoffman.

Writing that application was really hard. I always find it painful to revisit any of my past, whether talking about it or writing it down. Even now, writing this book brings up pain and tears and sadness. I have to be careful not to let these emotions consume me while I write. I have to be able to feel them and then let them pass through me. Fortunately, the therapy I engaged in after Martin's death, the Twelve Step meetings, and Hoffman all helped me learn to feel my emotions and to not shove them back down or ignore them. I discovered that it is okay to sit with anger or sadness for a while, but to not stay there. I learned that I need to feel in order to heal. Now I lean into the pain, acknowledge it, and use it to fuel my endeavors. But I wasn't there then.

In fact, leading up to my departure to Hoffman, I was a complete mess. My anxiety level was barely manageable. I feared the unknown. I feared being vulnerable around others. I was afraid that sharing even a few of the horrors from my past would crack the wall of my "I'm fine" defenses, allowing molten emotions to erupt in a devastating flood that would destroy me and everyone in their path. I was afraid of opening Pandora's box.

Since James had been to Hoffman, I tried to get him to tell me about the experience so it would not be so much of an unknown. I wanted to know what I was in for, but he knew that this would just make me more anxious. He also knew that part of my recovery involved learning how to stay outside my comfort zone; to not necessarily have my life planned out every single minute. Because I was a planner. That's how I make myself feel safe. I controlled my environment and that of my children. I didn't do anything without understanding all aspects of what was coming. I planned, researched, and then planned some more. But I couldn't plan for Hoffman—I couldn't control it—and that made it especially terrifying.

A Life-Changing Week

When the scary day finally arrived—March 1, 2014—my husband's stepmother was kind enough to pick me up from the airport in California and take me to the Hoffman grounds in Napa Valley. On the drive there, I was thankful for her company. She had been through the program, so it was comforting to have someone there with me who was familiar with what I was about to experience, even though she, like James, would not provide details. Despite her comforting presence, I was physically sick from anxiety the entire drive, second guessing my decision every single mile.

The expectation I had created was that I was going to be staying at a glamorous resort and that, in between the work we would be doing, I could get massages and relax. I envisioned Hoffman to be a spa where I could wear white robes and soft slippers. This fantasy made it way less threatening for me.

When we pulled up to the very humble accommodations, I turned to my stepmother-in-law and told her, "I am not doing this. I am not staying here." The grounds reminded me of the summer camp I used to go to when I was a child. It was small, secluded, and there was a row of rustic cabins along a creek. I remember wondering if they even had electricity or running water. That was an exaggeration, I know, but what I saw was nothing like the fantasy I had conjured in my mind. I felt betrayed, like I had been catfished. I immediately wanted to turn around and go home. I now know that my desire to flee had nothing to do with the accommodations and everything to do with the reality that I was actually here and that I would now have to go through with this. After we unloaded my bags, my step mother-in-law helped me check in, gave me a hug, and left me there with a reassuring look that said, "I've been there; you'll be okay."

One of the first things I had to do when I arrived at Hoffman was relinquish my cell phone. Phones are not allowed, but they were returned to us on the last day, right before we all departed. We were also not allowed to read anything other than approved material so as to not get distracted by the outside world. The program demanded our full and undivided attention because we were all there for a reason: we all had work to do.

I was assigned my cabin number and told to unpack and then gather in the dining room for a "meet and greet." I was so overwhelmed with both fear and relief that I just sat on my bed and cried. I did not feel like socializing. I did not feel like meeting new people. I was paralyzed with fear. But I also knew that if I did not stay, if I did not do this work, then I would be miserable the rest of my life. I knew that I did not have a choice. It was time to put my demons to rest. I wiped my tears and headed to the dining room.

I spent the next five days being the most uncomfortable I have ever been in my life. In the dining room, the forty of us were assigned to a group with ten participants and one counselor. Then all forty of us were instructed to make a large circle and hold hands. As I stood in that circle that first day, with forty strangers who all looked as lost as I was, I felt truly seen for the first time in my life. That terrified me, but it was also somewhat comforting.

Quietly, calmly, each counselor made their way around the circle, pausing in front of every single one of us. We had been instructed to look directly into their eyes when they approached us. This alone was an almost impossible task for me. My shame was too great to stare deeply into anyone's eyes for fear they would see my truth. But as the counselor who'd been assigned to my group came up to me, she gently took my hands and looked me directly in the eyes. She whispered the words, "I see you and I love you." I broke down into uncontrollable sobs. I knew, right then and there, that this program would save me.

As our five days progressed, sometimes we had group activities and sometimes we had sessions that we had to tackle individually. There were activities where I said to myself, "No way in hell am I doing that." But I did each and every single thing, no matter how uncomfortable or how much anxiety it created for me. I overcame every fear that came up, and I did everything they asked of me.

One of the many defining moments for me was during an experiential exercise designed to bring our anger to the surface so it could be released. This exercise involved a plastic whiffle bat and a pillow. This moment was life changing for me was because it taught me how to safely release my anger. It also brought to light the fact that I still had a lot of anger inside me, anger which

I thought I had addressed during the numerous times I went to "regular" therapy. Turns out, it had not all been addressed. We participated in these types of experiential exercises so many times over the week that I was completely exhausted by the time I left. But after releasing forty years of buried emotions, I no longer felt the weight of the world on my shoulders.

During a one-on-one session with my counselor, she told me she had not read a story quite like mine before and that she had coached at least a thousand people up to that point. Even though James would tell me that my story was not as normal as I made it out to be, it didn't really sink in until my counselor validated his words. That was the first time in my life that I thought, "Huh, maybe my story really is unique."

I'm not going to describe my time at Hoffman in great detail because they ask that we not reveal their process so as to not ruin the experience for others—or scare them away from attending at all. Suffice it to say that Hoffman saved me. It gave me a clean slate and the tools to function in a life that was now free from guilt, shame, and self-loathing. The heavy shadow that had followed and weighed me down, almost to the point where I could not move forward, was now lifted. The negative body image and self-hatred I was accustomed to was mostly gone. I was educated about abuse and my abusers. I had the opportunity to process the pain of my estrangement from my first-born son and the loss of the child I miscarried. The work I did there empowered me to quiet my anxiety, which has allowed me to try hard things. It helped rewire my brain so that my thinking and my thought process is now completely different than what I had been taught. This work gave me the ability to love myself so that I could be a better mother and a better wife. I finished the week with a brand-new confidence that I had never felt before.

I went into Hoffman with an entire lifetime of broken bricks that made up the foundation of my life. I came out of it with brand new bricks altogether. The old ones were discarded along with my demons. Hoffman was such an amazing and life changing experience that I did not even want my phone back on the last day; I did not want to leave the grounds. If I had the choice, I would have stayed there forever.

It's not uncommon for people to change so drastically during a week at Hoffman that they quit their jobs or leave their relationships. That's why the Hoffman leaders told us not to make any life changing decisions for at least ninety days after completing the program. They wanted to make sure we took the time to thoroughly process those types of decisions.

Before I went, my amazing husband explained to me that I would come out of the program a different person and that there was a chance I would not want to be married to him anymore. He told me he was willing to take that chance if it meant I could finally find inner peace and self-love. And he meant it. Luckily, I had no desire to leave James after Hoffman. Now that we have both gone through the program, we are connected on a much deeper level and our marriage is even stronger.

There is one event from our married life that illustrates the depth of the healing that I experienced at Hoffman. In 2018, when we moved into our new house, James and I went shopping for all new kitchen appliances and everything else imaginable. Given that Norman had chased me out of my childhood home with a butcher knife, and what had happened with Martin, and then with Mike, I would not allow a butcher block, or any knives larger than a steak knife, in my home after my marriage to Mike. Just the sight of a butcher knife crippled me with fear and caused me to have a severe physical reaction. After Hoffman, this reaction was more manageable. I agreed to let James buy a butcher block and a complete set of knives for our new home, including a butcher knife. He is very careful with it around me, and knows that I am always aware of its presence. Every time someone pulls that butcher knife out of its block I am still transported back to that horrific day with Martin, but I have learned how to maneuver through the feelings that come up.

Hoffman didn't completely cure everything. That's not realistic. But what was left was manageable.

My Way… But Not the Only Way

While Hoffman, Twelve-Step programs, and therapy are the paths I initially followed to healing and recovery, please know that they are certainly not the only avenues. If you are wanting to change your life, your path does not have to be expensive, nor do you do need to enroll in a week-long program, or go to the extremes that I did. Today, there are so many options for you if you are looking to rewire the negative messaging you have received throughout your life. As the Buddhists say, "When the student is ready, the teacher will come."

It's also important to understand that you alone have the power to change your life. Yes, I have been very fortunate to have a loving husband who has supported me on this journey and even pointed me in the direction of some roads to recovery. Nevertheless, I was the one who had to decide to go down those roads. I was the one who had to face my fears, power through my anxieties, and do the hard work of healing. And so can you.

No matter where you choose to begin, the most important thing is to love yourself enough to realize that you are worth it. Then, watch for the paths that open before you… and start taking those first steps.

PART SIX

THE ROAD OF HEALING
THROUGH FITNESS

TWENTY ONE

Finding My Passion

"If there is no passion in your life, then have you really lived?
Find your passion, whatever it may be.
Become it, and let it become you and you will find
great things happen for you, to you and because of you."

--Alan Armstrong

Hoffman gave me a jumpstart to healing and the tools I needed to create a healthy, happy life. Now it was up to me to make sure I used those tools and took advantage of that jumpstart.

One of the tools I got from Hoffman were "gratitude walks" which I eventually turned into "gratitude runs." With every step, I would state something I was grateful for. With every mile, I would circulate positive thoughts and gratitude. It was impossible to be in a bad mood when I finished a gratitude run. These runs gave me a better way to manage stress and the remaining anxiety I still had from time to time. To this day, I still use this practice, especially if I am having a particularly rough time.

Another tool I got from Hoffman was the realization that I was so much more than others had told me I was. I was armed with the idea that I could do hard things. Now I wanted to push myself to see what I could accomplish. I was willing to try new things, even though I would have to work through my fears and risk failure to see what I could do.

Endurance Sports

Prior to Hoffman, James and I had done some recreational running here and there, nothing more than three or four miles. It was an activity we both enjoyed, and we enjoyed doing it together. But I never had the courage to push myself beyond those few miles. I had always wanted to run a half marathon, but never believed in myself enough to try. I had always wanted to run a full marathon, but I needed to complete a half before attempting a full. Equipped with my new tools from Hoffman, I decided that the spring of 2017 was when I would run my first half marathon. I found a simple training plan online and began my journey.

I am not a fast runner, so instead of concerning myself with my pace, I set a goal of finishing that half marathon with as little walking as possible. The plan I was using incorporated four days of running with a long run on the weekend and two days of cross training. I would go to the gym and do strength training with weights or even utilize the elliptical as a break from pounding the pavement day after day. My running mechanics were off. As an overpronator, I was running in the wrong shoes, so I kept struggling with injuries. But I persevered. I did not miss a training day unless I was dealing with an injury. When I could finally run ten miles, I was elated! I had never thought I could run so far! Accomplishing what I had previously seen as an unachievable goal built up my confidence and greatly improved the way I thought about myself and my capabilities.

I competed in the local half marathon on April 8, 2017, and came in nineth in my age group. I did not have a fast time—two hours and seventeen minutes—but I ran the entire distance without walking. The only issue I had was around mile ten. Coming up a nasty hill, I thought I was going to vomit. I hit the wall because I had foolishly not taken in any nutrition. Fruit and pastries were being handed out around mile eight, but I felt fine, so I did not eat anything. I never trained with gels or food and was not educated on the importance of nutrition in endurance sports. I pulled off to the side of the road in anticipation of the upheaval, but the nausea quickly subsided, and I continued the race. At mile twelve I got dizzy. Because my body was now running on fumes, I know I could not have gone any further that day than the required 13.1 miles, but I accomplished what I set out to do.

When I crossed the finish line, I told my husband that I could not imagine having to do that distance all over again—referring to a full marathon. He laughed and said, "You're going to want to do a full marathon next." He was right. He knows me well, even better than I know myself sometimes. About a month later I announced to him that, in 2018, I wanted to run a full marathon.

My First Marathon

James had a friend whose wife coached athletes, so he agreed to pay her to coach me across the finish line of my first marathon. This was a huge step for me. The thought of tackling a marathon was overwhelming, and frightening, and exciting. Since I only had four months to train for this event, my coach immediately began to outline structured weekly workouts for me.

During these four months I had to overcome one injury after another. I had issues with my IT band, plantar fasciitis, turf toe, and right before the event, I started getting pain on the top of my foot. I believe most of these injuries came from the fact that I was still trying to run in neutral shoes and I am not a neutral runner. I also had poor mechanics back then—something I still work on every time I run, which has greatly improved my form. I was icing, heating, massaging, and doing anything I could to keep my body from falling apart so I could do that marathon. I had spent so much time training that not running it was not an option. Unfortunately, the pain in my foot was increasing to the point where I could not complete the final speed runs and tempo runs two weeks out from the event. I had to pull back and baby my foot in the hope that it would not get worse.

The difficulties of these physical challenges were matched by the mental battles I had to wage every time I attempted to run further than the thirteen miles I already knew I could do. The idea of running fifteen, seventeen, or twenty miles was a daunting prospect for my mind and body to embrace. I battled my Dark Side daily as it continued to tell me, "You can't do this." I found positive mantras to replace the dark voice and, little by little, it got quieter. My Dark Side still comes around from time to time, and that will always be the case. But I've learned that continually replacing its voice with positive messages is the real key to shutting it down.

When the day of the marathon arrived, I was ready—physically and mentally. Having learned my lesson regarding nutrition and fueling, I made sure that, this time, I had enough of both to get me through. My husband met me about every five miles with an electrolyte drink and food. This way I didn't have to stop at the aid stations and risk upsetting my stomach by taking in nourishment that may be different from what I had been training with. My coach was also riding her bicycle along the course, checking in on me from time to time.

I was in good spirits and doing well the first fifteen miles. Clicking right along at the pace my coach had outlined for me, I was sticking to the plan. It was cold and I had multiple layers on, including gloves. Parts of the course were windy, and it was brutal at times, but I was managing the hills and the weather up to this point.

Then came mile seventeen. I was already slowing down, both from fatigue and because my foot had been hurting worse and worse as the miles wore on. I had taped it thoroughly before the race in the hope that, between the adhesive and the adrenaline, it would hold up. Not only had my pace slowed considerably, but my mind was all over the place. Music helped me focus when I ran. It also gave me that added burst when I needed it. What I did not plan for was the battery limitations on my smart watch, which is where my music was stored.

At mile seventeen everything fell apart. My watch died on me when I most needed my music and the ability to see my pacing. This was a tough break because I still had nine miles to go and because my mind was turning on me. To make matters worse, about a mile or so before that mark I felt a sharp pain in the foot I was already babying. It began to hurt in a way that was significantly different than the unpleasantness I had been experiencing up until this point. Every step I took was now incredibly painful. I began questioning if I could even complete the required 26.2 miles with this injury.

The first set of tears came when I hit mile twenty. I had heard that runners often experience a burst of adrenaline at that point because they realize they are almost done. But I never got the rush that was supposed to carry me through those last six miles. I was hurting too badly.

My coach was waiting for me at mile twenty and had planned on running the last six miles with me to keep me motivated and to make sure I made it across the finish line. When I saw her waiting for me, I stopped, and the tears immediately began to fall. In between the tears of defeat, I explained to her what was happening with my foot and that I no longer had my music. Grabbing her phone, she put on some of my favorite songs, gave me a few words of encouragement, and off we went.

I had to stop at just about every aid station now. I was hurting so badly that I needed the quick break. I was just trying to get through one mile at a time. The second time I cried was at mile twenty-three when I saw my husband. He was going to run the last three miles with me and my coach. He was exactly what I needed to get my ass through those last thirty minutes. I cried some more, gave him a hug, and off we went.

The last mile I was suffering so badly I did not even want them to talk to me, so they quietly jogged behind me as I labored on. They pulled off the last few hundred feet as I victoriously crossed that finish line. The tears fell again, but this time they were tears of joy and relief. It was ugly, and not how I wanted my first marathon experience to be, but I finished, and I did not give up. I did not quit. I persevered, earning more sturdy bricks to help me rebuild the way I thought about myself.

Unfortunately, I did fall into my old patterns for a bit. I finished the race in five hours, twenty-one minutes, and fifteen seconds (5:21:15), missing my goal of coming in under five hours. I have yet to break the pattern of being incredibly hard on myself, so even though completing this race was an enormous accomplishment, I beat myself up over my finish time. Instead of allowing myself to bask in the glow of my achievement—finishing my first marathon—while injured!—all I could focus on was my perceived failure. (Come to find out, I had a stress fracture in my foot. I was in a boot for six to eight weeks after the marathon.)

After I stopped beating up on myself, I realized I had learned something incredibly important from completing this marathon; I learned how strong I really am. I learned I can do very hard things. I realized that the abusers in my past who had called me "weak" or told me, "You're not good enough" were wrong. I now knew I could accomplish whatever I set my mind to.

I had thought I would set my mind to training to do better in my next marathon. But I soon found myself on another path, something far more grueling than a marathon.

Ironman Dreams

My first introduction to Ironman came while I was training for my first running events. I had no idea what a triathlon or an Ironman was. When I saw the Ironman World Championships in Kona on a television at the gym, I was blown away. I thought a marathon alone was tough, but an Ironman required swimming 2.4 miles using a formal freestyle stroke, cycling 112 miles, and then running 26.2 miles—a full marathon! Each leg had to be completed in the same day, back-to-back, and you had to finish within seventeen hours or you did not get a medal. You did not get those bragging rights. All you got was a big fat DNF next to your name: Did Not Finish. I quietly told myself that I wanted to try this. I wanted to be someone who crossed that finish line and did this very, very hard thing.

My Dark Side immediately convinced me it was unachievable. "What? Are you kidding me? You barely finished that marathon, you've had little experience with cycling, and you don't even know how to do that freestyle swim stroke. Nope, this is for other people. This is not something you can do." I packed this dream away and did not mention it to my husband or anyone else for another whole year.

In October of 2018, I was sitting on our couch at home, again watching the Ironman World Championships in Kona. I had become a real closet fan of the sport and made a point of not missing the live broadcast of this annual event. My husband was watching with me when I made the mistake of musing aloud, "Finishing a full Ironman would be a dream come true."

He immediately looked at me and said, "You should do it."

Hearing all this, my Dark Side quickly chimed in with its relentless refrain, "No, you can't do that. You can't swim freestyle and you're a horrible cyclist. You're crazy and stupid for even thinking you could tackle something so tough."

Over my Dark Side's objections, I could see the wheels turning in my husband's head. I knew he was about to go all in on this. James has always been—and still is—my biggest fan. He always supports and encourages me to conquer anything I want to tackle. And back then, he had way more confidence in me than I had in myself.

Cowed into submission by my Dark Side, I tried to rationalize with James. I explained that I didn't know how to swim freestyle, that I was too old to learn, that it was just too overwhelming, and . . . blah, blah blah, blah, blah. One excuse after another came falling out of my mouth. It's not that I didn't want to try this; it's that fear was taking over and controlling my thought process.

James told me that he would pay for a coach and anything else I needed to make sure I became an Ironman, just as he had done when I wanted to run a marathon. He was adamant. "We will spend however much money is needed and do whatever it takes to make this happen."

In that moment, I decided to not let fear win.

"All right," I said, "Let's do this." I was excited, nervous, scared, anxious, and elated—all at the same time! I knew this was going to be a long journey, and I desperately wanted to take it.

When I told the coach who had gotten me over my marathon finish line about this new goal, she said, "This will be a one- or two-years-long venture." She explained that it would be best to start with smaller, local triathlons, and then work my way up to a half Ironman in 2019. She also recommended undertaking the half Ironman (70.3 miles) later the following year to give me as much time as possible to train for it. My coach helped me choose a few local events to compete in and learn from. Then we decided that the October 2019 Ironman Waco would be my first big target.

And so it began. My training started with the most challenging thing I have ever had to learn: the freestyle swim stroke. I did nothing but swallow water for the first three weeks! I couldn't even get through a lap in the pool. It was exhausting. For months I felt like I would never get the hang of it. I watched hours and hours of YouTube videos on form and I would practice three- to four-times a week. I eventually got to the point where I was somewhat mimicking the freestyle stroke . . . slowly . . . but I was doing it! All it took was tons of work, perseverance, grit, and determination.

TWENTY TWO

The Diagnosis

The Devil whispered, "You can't withstand the storm."
I replied . . . "I am the storm."
– Sarvesh Kulkarni

"Your boobs are too small. You ought to get breast implants." Martin told me this over and over when we were married. On top of all the rest of my body image issues, I now felt insecure about my small breasts. We could never afford this kind of elective surgery when he was alive, but his taunts stuck with me. In 2004, a year after Martin died, I decided to get those implants. My broken mind told me that no man would want me if I didn't do everything I could to fix my physical self. Besides—and I'm not going to lie here—I was so angry at Martin for the mess he left me in that part of me wanted to get the implants just to give him the finger.

At the recommendation of my doctor, I went for the D cups. He told me that with my height and frame I could carry those off beautifully—and I did.

A Ruptured Breast Implant

In November of 2018, I woke up one morning to find I had lopsided breasts. One of my implants had ruptured. I wasn't completely surprised. They had far exceeded their expiration date. I had known it was just a matter of time before I would need to do something about them.

When this happened, I had just started training to become a triathlete. The large D breast implants were more of a hindrance now than anything else. As an athlete, I liked the idea of a flat chest. I was ready to have them out.

If my implants had been silicone, the toxic substance leaking into my body would have created a medical emergency. But my implants were saline, so the rupture was not considered a medical emergency. This meant my insurance would not cover anything related to them. Whatever James and I decided to do, we would have to pay for the entire procedure.

My doctor outlined three options for me. The first option was to have the implants surgically removed and have a lift done with what was left. I really liked that idea, but that procedure came with a whopping $8,000 bill. That option suddenly became a non-option. The second option was to have the implants surgically removed in a hospital under anesthesia. That option cost around $4,000. This was a bit more manageable, but still a lot of money for us at the time. The third option the doctor gave me, but did not recommend, was to have the implants removed in his office by just numbing my breasts with a local anesthetic. He could do this for the bargain price of $2,500. The only reason this third possibility was even an option is because, when I initially got the implants, they had been placed over my muscle and not underneath it. Consequently, my doctor could simply make a couple of slits under each breast and pull them out.

My husband would have spent the $8,000 if I had asked him to. James would do anything for me that was within his power to do. But I did not want to spend that kind of money. Even after Hoffman, and regularly attending a Twelve-Step program, and all the recovery I had experienced, I still had trouble accepting the fact that I was worth it. So, I chose option number three. Yes, it wasn't recommended by the doctor, but I knew I was tough. I knew I could suffer through a procedure if it saved us a ton of money.

James travels a lot for his job. He was going to be out of town the week of my appointment, but once again, my mom was there for me. I am so glad she was because the procedure did not go as planned. The implants had been in my body for so long that they had adhered to pieces of me. After the incisions were made under each breast, my implants did not slip out easily as predicted. The doctor later told me he would have never gone that route if he had known this was going to be the case. He would have insisted on surgery and had me comfortably asleep. It took the doctor and two nurses to pull out each implant. Needless to say, this was highly traumatic and extremely painful for me. But I powered through it, like I always powered through things, and went home with my mom to rest.

I thought this would be the end of it. Little did I know, this was only the beginning.

Biopsies and a Personal Record (PR)

When the swelling from this traumatic procedure finally went down, I noticed a lump in my right breast. It was so high on top of my breast that it was almost not on my breast at all. Since I had my annual mammogram appointment already scheduled for a few days later, I mentioned it when they were taking pictures, but nothing showed up. Unbeknownst to me, my tissue was too dense for the mammogram to pick up the mass, so my report came back "normal."

Because of my normal report, at first, I was not worried. I showed my husband the lump, and he was not worried. We both assumed that it was just scar tissue from the rough procedure I had undergone several weeks earlier. Since my annual exam with my OB was coming up the following month, I set aside all thoughts of this lump. I figured I'd let my OB examine it when I saw her.

I'll never forget that appointment. It was the first of many where my heart stopped; where everything stopped.

As soon as I saw my OB, she had a look of concern on her face. "You need to have an ultrasound to have that looked at right away. I will get that scheduled." I argued with her, explaining it was just scar tissue from having my implants removed.

The first time my heart stopped was when she responded, "I don't think so."

This time I made sure to schedule the ultrasound for when my husband would be in town so he could go with me. This was one appointment where I needed him to be there for me in case it went in the wrong direction. I was not going to tell anyone else about these appointments until I had a definite answer either way. The last thing I needed was everyone around me to freak out because I was doing a fine job of that all on my own!

I worried and obsessed, day and night, waiting for my appointment. My husband has a friend who is a surgeon. This friend reassured James that most of the time these lumps are benign. Since I had no history of breast cancer in my family, he said, "You don't need to be concerned. The odds of this being something more than a harmless mass are low." Obviously, he did not know my life story because this is exactly the kind of thing that happens to me.

On appointment day, once the ultrasound was finished, James and I had to sit in an office and wait. I swear I did not breathe the entire time we were waiting for the doctor to come give us the results. I could see the worry on my husband's face. He tried to be strong for me, but I saw just how concerned he was.

Finally, a doctor who barely looked old enough to drive arrived to give us the pre-diagnosis. "We're pretty sure it's breast cancer."

My heart stopped again. My world stopped.

James and I both went into shock. The rest of what she said sounded like, "Blah, blah, blah . . . and you will need a biopsy and a follow up MRI to confirm the diagnosis and determine if there are more masses in either breast."

James and I had driven in separate vehicles. I vividly remember sitting in my car, in the parking lot. I broke down and cried. This was the second most terrifying day I have ever experienced--and I had gone through a lot up until now. All I could think about was my older son, my daughter, and my two little boys. I feared my younger sons would not make it if I died from cancer and they were forced to go live with their alcoholic dad. And I certainly did not want to die. I had a lot of shit I wanted to do, and this seemed so unfair! I eventually had to go through the grieving process, but at this point, all I was experiencing was pure fear.

I still insisted that we not tell anyone until we had the final lab results from the biopsy. James agreed, so we kept it to ourselves as we scheduled the first biopsy and MRI appointments.

By the time we followed the process, made the appointments, and got to the day that I was to have my first biopsy, it was the day before I was to run a half marathon. I had been training diligently for it, in preparation for my first triathlon and half Ironman 70.3 event, and I was certainly not going to let a biopsy get in my way of completing any of them.

The biopsy was painful but bearable. The doctor was not a fan of me running the next day but luckily, she too was a runner, so she knew the mentality that came along with the sport. She made me promise that I would quit if I started to bleed. I agreed, of course. Anything to get her blessing—as if I would not have run it even if she told me I couldn't. I just felt better being able to tell James and my coach that the doctor said it was fine to run the half marathon. I absolutely had no intention of stopping if I started bleeding either. That was a little white lie I allowed myself to tell her. I ran the next morning and PR'd (personal record) the race by twenty minutes. I came in seventh in my age group and was very pleased with myself.

After the high of doing so well in my race, I faced the low of a weeklong wait for the lab results from my mass to come back. They were "pretty sure" I had breast cancer, but these lab results would confirm things and give the doctor an idea of what kind of tumor we were facing. That had to have been the longest week of my life!

I told my boss what was going on, in confidence, because I needed to work remotely and take some time for myself. I was too distracted to put much effort into my job. I could not control my emotions.

The Saturday after my half marathon, I got the call saying that it was indeed breast cancer. I was also told I had to go back in and have my left breast biopsied as they found a "few areas of concern" from the MRI. They would not be able to determine what stage I was in until they removed the tumor and the lymph nodes around it and conducted additional lab work to see if the cancer had spread to the closest lymph nodes. I would not know the severity of my situation until I had a surgery to remove the invading enemy.

As scary as all this was, I was also experiencing a deep sense of gratitude. I had realized that, despite my commitment to monthly breast self-exams, yearly mammograms, and OB checkups, my lump could not be felt because it sat underneath my implant, which sat on top of my breast muscle and tissue. The lump could not be seen by a mammogram due to the density of my tissue. If my implant had not ruptured, I probably would have never found that lump until it was too late. I had no doubt that finding it as early as I did was giving me a fighting chance. For me, this was another "God Deal." I firmly believe my guardian angel popped that implant herself so I would find that tumor. This would be my fifth brush with death, and I knew my angel was right there, fighting with me and for me.

TWENTY THREE

Treatments and Triathlons

"Life doesn't get easier or more forgiving;
we get stronger and more resilient."

--Dr. Steve Maraboli

Time to Fight Again

My first decision regarding treatment was asked of me at this point. Did I want a lumpectomy to just remove the tumor, or did I want a mastectomy or even a double mastectomy?

My surgeon told me it was a personal decision and she would support whatever route I chose to take. If I opted for the lumpectomy, I would have to follow that with radiation and possibly chemo if my labs showed any sign of spread. If I opted for a partial or a full mastectomy, I was looking at serious down time and more than one reconstruction surgery. Then, if there were signs of spreading, I would still have to undergo chemotherapy but not radiation as all the breast tissue would have been removed.

My first thought was, "I have a race season coming up. I have the Waco 70.3 Ironman to complete. I am not going to let cancer get in the way of either of these goals." It wasn't an easy decision, and I weighed the pros and cons of each option. Like my surgeon, James also said it was my decision. He encouraged me to do what I thought was right for me.

I do not have breast cancer on either side of my family, but because I did not know my father's side of the family very well, I decided to have the genetic testing done just to be sure I did not have the Her2 gene. The Her2 gene means that the cancer is hereditary, and it tends to spread more rapidly. The results of this test would help inform my treatment decisions. If I had the Her2 gene, or if the biopsies done on the other breast came out positive for cancer, I would opt for a full mastectomy. Luckily, both of these things came back negative, so it made my options clearer.

I decided to go ahead with the lumpectomy and the radiation. If my labs came back that I needed chemo, well . . . I would do that too. I was ready for the fight.

Triathlon Camp

My surgeon wanted me to have the lumpectomy as soon as possible so we could know what type of tumor we were dealing with and what stage of cancer I was in. She scheduled the surgery for the first available date, but that date was not acceptable to me. That date was for one week before triathlon camp.

When I got my breast cancer diagnosis, I had only been training as a triathlete for several months. My coach had told me about two great opportunities: becoming part of an endurance team—a group that creates workouts and organizes communal running, swimming, and biking outings to help motivate members to train—and triathlon camp. I had joined an endurance team, but had yet to meet any of its members. Tri camp would give me this opportunity. Since I had already signed up for camp, I was determined to not miss out on a weekend of training, learning, and finally getting to know my endurance teammates.

After my surgery, I was going to be down for a short time and would not have been able to attend camp. That's why I insisted on a different date for the lumpectomy. My surgeon reluctantly agreed to move it out until the Monday following tri camp weekend. This is not the first time she and I would debate such things. I frequently had to convince her to let me get back to training much sooner than she would have preferred.

While I desperately wanted to attend tri camp, I was also absolutely terrified about going. My anxiety had decreased significantly after Hoffman, and I was certainly more willing to try new things, but that didn't mean I never had to face fears. I was purposely doing things that scared me, but I still got extremely anxious when playing outside my comfort zone. I was already in a fragile emotional state, knowing what was waiting for me on the other side of that weekend. Mix that emotional state with the anxiety of facing new people and doing new things, and well . . . let's just say I was a bit of a hot mess internally. It's a good thing I had learned how to mask my true emotions. I still had that skill in my toolbox. It was a skill I had sharpened over many, many years, and one that still came in handy from time to time.

My anxiety was heightened by the fact that, along with not knowing anyone, I would be spending the entire weekend at a lodge where I would be sharing a room with not just one—or two, or even three—but with four other women! Then there was the fact that I had been riding on a bike trainer these past few months, and this would be the first time I was getting my new tri bike out on the road. I had also just bought new clip-in cleats and was still learning how to clip in and out on the bike. Oh! And let's not forget that I had never used my hard-to-learn swim stroke outside a pool before!

Everything at tri camp felt like a brand-new experience to me, but it was also one of the best experiences I've ever had. What I learned that weekend was vital to me as a new triathlete. I learned so much about myself and about what I could overcome. I accomplished workouts that, going into them, my mind told me, "There's no way you're going to be able to do that." But I did! I may not have been the fastest in the group, but I completed the challenges that were presented. The confidence I gained that weekend was so important. I needed it going into my surgery, going into my treatments, and going into my first races as a triathlete. More than ever, I needed validation that I could do hard things. And that's just what I got at tri camp.

I only fell twice trying to unclip from my bike. Both times, we were almost at a stand-still. Both times, there was a large group of more experienced athletes watching me. Of course, I was mortified with each tumble. But everyone was so supportive! They acted like it was no big deal. I now understand that it really isn't a big deal. Even the most seasoned athlete makes a misstep with a cleat every now and then, and down they go.

I also didn't do the open water swim in the lake in its entirety.

Okay, I didn't do any of it, but I did hang out with a couple of other newbies in the cove. We practiced putting our heads in the freezing, murky water, and we swam a little bit, just to get used to it. The next day, we swam a little farther. It was only April, so the water was unbelievably cold—fifty-seven degrees, to be exact! When I went to put my face in the water, it took my breath away. I was like, "Nope! Not going to do that!" I eventually did, and I eventually got over that fear. Now I can swim in a cold lake and it doesn't faze me much. I was grateful to have a couple other team-mates that were also struggling with this. I was in good company, and we had fun as we conquered the cold water.

Throughout the weekend, I had managed to keep my emotions in check and power through the workouts and the unknowns—with my cancer diagnosis and upcoming surgery still weighing heavily on my mind. I was doing well until I started climbing what shall forever be known to me as "Cry Baby Hill."

All weekend, I was having issues keeping up with everyone on my bike. At first, I didn't think anything of it because I was not a particularly strong cyclist and I had never had my race bike out on the road. I was learning how to control it in the aero position and learning the gearing. But on this particular day, I began getting frustrated with myself for continually falling behind. And then we came to Cry Baby Hill.

My coach finally had to circle back and find me. I was some-where on the hill by myself, barely getting up it. I was on the verge of tears and hating on myself. My Dark Side was screaming in my ear, "You do not belong here!" I was struggling to ignore it, but rapidly losing that mental battle.

My coach heard something scraping on my bike, and said she thought my brake was rubbing. She told me she'd look at it at the top of the hill; I just needed to get to the top. Unable to hold back the tears any longer, I began to cry. I was afraid of the future. I was angry. I was frustrated. I was tired. My tears were partly due to that dreadful hill but mostly due to my cancer diagnosis. My coach sensed a breakdown coming and yelled back at me, "You are not allowed to cry on this hill! You must get up this hill because, if you stop, you will have to walk it. You can cry and breakdown all you want when you get to the top of this hill."

My coach was the only person at camp that knew my situation. She was not unsympathetic; she was just trying to get my ass up that hill! It worked. I stopped crying, dug in, and finally made it to the top. I climbed off my bike and then proceeded to have a full-on meltdown.

I needed that breakdown. I needed to let it all out and have that release of emotions. That hill was a safe place. Everyone else was on their way back to the lodge, so no one was the wiser.

My coach kept her promise and allowed me all the time I needed to cry. She checked out my brake which had, indeed, been rubbing the whole time I was trying to climb. Cycling back to the team house was a far better experience. I felt better mentally, and the bike was moving much easier now that my coach had fixed my brake.

That was a rough day, but this has become one of my favorite stories to tell. Now I can laugh about that day on Cry Baby Hill.

Confidence and Recovery

When the surgeon did my lumpectomy, she also removed a cluster of my lymph nodes to test to see if the cancer had spread. Those results would determine whether chemotherapy was going to be added to my treatment plan.

When I learned that my lymph nodes were clean, relief, joy and gratitude flooded through my body. There was no sign of cancer; no sign of spreading. This was the first time, going through this process, when I began to feel confident that I was going to survive another battle; confident that I was going to be allowed to live longer and be here for my children; confident that I was not going to be taken away from my husband, my best friend.

I had the lumpectomy surgery in May of 2019. My very first triathlon was scheduled for just one month later, June 2019. I had been training as much as possible after the surgery, although not nearly at the level I desired. I was completely down for a couple of days, but began walking around my third day. My surgeon had told me it would be good for me to walk. What she failed to understand is that her idea of walking and my idea were two totally different things. Her idea of walking was taking a nice leisurely stroll through my neighborhood. My idea was doing five or six miles at a fast pace. One day, I even walked a very challenging workout, my hill repeat workout, since I could not yet run it. I was having regular check-ups with my surgeon. When she realized I was not going to stay down or follow the standard post surgery exercise plan, she conceded and outlined something we both could live with. My surgeon told me that one thing she had learned as a doctor is that mental health is a big part of recovery. If my mental health was tied to training, then she would allow me to do it—with some restrictions, of course.

I mostly followed her instructions, but I pushed it harder than she probably wanted me to. I knew my body. I knew where and when I could push it. I am also certain that she knew I was going to push. I was jogging and on my bike trainer the second week of recovery, swimming and running my third week of recovery, and competed in my very first triathlon the fourth week of recovery.

I was not about to miss this race, especially since I was getting ready to begin a month of radiation treatments. Every single day I was going to have to go for these treatments, and I knew they were going to wipe out my energy. This race was going to be my very first triathlon, and I did not want to miss out on my chance to be a triathlete.

My First Triathlon

The triathlon was a local event. It was a shorter course with a swim of one thousand yards, a nineteen-mile bike ride, and a four-mile run. It's what is called an international distance. I felt confident about the bike and the run, but swimming was my Achille's heel. I had just learned how to swim that year, and I was not a strong swimmer, I was not a fast swimmer, and I was not a confident swimmer. When I first began to learn how to freestyle swim, I did nothing but swallow water for three weeks. The first time I attempted to swim twenty-five yards, I barely made it. I thought to myself, "This is such bullshit! Swimming sucks!" My open water swimming was an even worse spectacle than swimming in a pool. I would get so anxious before an open water swim session at the lake that my stomach would be in knots the entire day leading up to it. This race had an open water swim, and I was petrified of the thousand yards I had to conquer.

The day before the event, my coach met me and another woman from our endurance team at the lake where the race was going to take place. Since we both struggled with swimming, our goal was to swim a couple hundred yards around the buoys without panicking. I needed to practice keeping my heart from not beating out of my chest in open water. I knew I would need to remain calm on race day. If my breathing got out of whack, the swim would prove to be very difficult.

We waded out into the swimming area and then swam out to the swim buoys and gave it a go. We only swam three- to four-hundred yards, and it wasn't horrible. Coming back in, we were tired and started to get a little panicked. That's when our coach yelled, "Stand up!" We had no idea we were already in the shallow end! The kids playing in the adjacent swimming area found this amusing, which made us laugh at ourselves even more. It was a small win that day, and a sense of accomplishment washed over me, literally. I gained just enough confidence from that short swim to get me through the one thousand yards the next day. Even though I was extremely nervous, I did not suffer a meltdown. I was able to keep my heart rate in check.

Going into this race, I wasn't even sure if I would like doing a triathlon. While I had always loved running, I was only a fair cyclist, and my swimming skills left much to be desired. After registering for these few local events and the Ironman Waco 70.3, I committed to myself that I would complete these races even if I did not particularly enjoy the sport.

But that was not the case. I loved triathlon! What thrilled me was the challenge of conquering three sports at once and the organization required for the transitions. The planning it takes to ensure I had properly lined up all my gear, hydration, and nutrition fed right into my obsessive planning traits. I loved every aspect of it! Yes, I still hated swimming, but since I liked being challenged, I was motivated to overcome my fear of the water and improve my speed. This first triathlon was not my fastest race that year, but because it was a smaller event, and not crowded, I ended up getting first place in my age group. That was it! From that moment on, I was all in.

I was signed up for two other local triathlons that summer, but first I had to undergo my radiation treatments and start my hormone therapy. The next triathlon was not for a month, just about the time when I would complete my radiation. I was told this was when I would probably be at my worst physically. I was warned about extreme fatigue, nauseousness, and open wounds on my chest from the radiation burns. My oncologist instructed me not to open water swim if I had open wounds. This meant that I would not be able to do my next triathlon if my burns blistered. I kept my fingers crossed!

Training Through Radiation Treatments

I trained just about every day when I was going through my daily radiation treatments. My coach stayed in tune with how I was feeling, and we would dial back the training as needed. I pushed myself because I was determined to not lose ground on my fitness. I was determined to defeat the cancer and get my life back.

I was determined to complete the 70.3 Ironman because it was a stepping-stone on the way to fulfilling my dream of finishing a full 140.6 Ironman.

My oncologist quickly learned just how stubborn I was. He, too, realized he was not going to be able to keep me down. Just as my surgeon had done, he loosened my restrictions based on how I was feeling. He let me train as my body was up to it.

I began my radiation treatments in June of 2019. My treatment plan consisted of me going in every day for almost a month to get zapped. The side effects are usually delayed about two weeks. I was informed by my doctor that the worst of it would be after I had finished, and that I would begin feeling the effects about a week after I started the process.

Being off work until my surgery and all treatments were completed, my days consisted of going in for my radiation in the morning, training as much as I could, and at least one nap—but most days I needed two. The procedure itself wasn't bad, although there were days that I felt nauseous right after. It made training, especially swimming, quite challenging. Most days I could push through the nausea and the fatigue, but there were a couple of days when I was so wiped out that I could not make it off the couch.

I did not like going into the Cancer Center because it was a daily reminder that I was sick. I was extremely grateful that I did not need chemotherapy. Every time I went to the clinic, I almost felt guilty that I got to just pass by the chemo rooms. I'm not sure how I would have managed training if I'd had to go through what those patients were experiencing. I could tell they were suffering greatly. My heart ached for them and at the same time, I felt silent gratitude that I did not have to join them. Whenever I would get down about what I was going through, I reminded myself that it could be a whole lot worse.

I was by far the youngest person I had seen at the facility. My oncologist would brag on me saying, "She's not the typical patient I see." His son was a triathlete, so we always had something in common to chat about at my appointments. In fact, his son talked him into doing a short course triathlon, and near the end of my treatments, he started training for it. My oncologist understood the work triathlon required. He knew how important it was to me.

As I approached the end of my radiation therapy, there were days I tried to complete my training, but I would end up in tears instead. I was so ready for the fatigue to be over. I was relieved to think that I would soon get my energy back. It was hard on my oncologist to have to break it to me that the hormone therapy I would need after completing my radiation therapy would wipe me out just as badly, if not worse, than the radiation. I was devastated when he explained that I would be fighting low energy levels for quite some time to come—maybe even years. I could not imagine my hormone therapy wiping me out more than the radiation had. I was certain my doctor had to be mistaken about that.

My radiation treatments ended on July 2, 2019. My chest was red and blistered, but it was done. My blisters had not opened up, so I was still clear to swim in the lake.

The next step in my regimen was to shut off my estrogen, so I started taking hormone drugs immediately following my radiation treatments. My tumor was estrogen positive, so I had a higher chance of staying in remission if my body wasn't feeding the damn thing. As my oncologist had predicted, the hormone therapy was worse than the radiation. My body fought it and refused to obey. My body was not going to shut down with just a daily pill.

After a month of not being successful with just the Tamoxifen, my oncologist wanted to inject me in the stomach every month with a shot of something that cost $1,200. This shot was not only painful in my stomach; it was painful in the pocketbook! My insurance company fought paying for this treatment for quite some time. After three injections, I almost did not receive any more shots because my bill had not been resolved. My doctor sent numerous letters explaining the need for the injections. Finally, the insurance company ponied up.

The even bigger problem with these injections is that yes, they worked, but they absolutely tanked my energy. It was so bad my doctor and I agreed that I would not get a shot in October, the month I was scheduled to do the 70.3 half Ironman in Waco, Texas. He said that, if I had that injection, I wouldn't have the energy to even get through the course. He gave me a shot every month except October, as promised. It was small miracle that I had enough energy to compete that day.

TWENTY FOUR

Outside My Comfort Zone

"Step outside your comfort zone because
that's the only way you're going to grow."
--Madeline Brewer

Competing in my first half Ironman meant something different to me after my breast cancer diagnosis. Sure, I wanted to prove to myself that I could do this very hard thing, and I needed to complete a half so I could move on to a full Ironman. But still… just a few short months before the race, I was not even sure I was going to be alive to compete. I was not sure what stage of cancer I was in, if I needed chemotherapy, or if I'd be too sick to train. The Waco Half Ironman became extremely emotional for me and for James. For us, this was going to be the ultimate "Fuck you!" to my breast cancer.

I was so touched by the support of my family and my endurance teammates. One of my teammates found a picture of the bridge we would be crossing at the finish line in Waco. He had a saying added to it: Believe in yourself, push your limits, and you will conquer your goals. I hung that up in my pain cave as a constant reminder for me to believe in myself.

My "pain cave" was a workout room James had created for me in my daughter's bedroom when she moved into her own apartment. It started with a weight area with mats, a spot for my bike and trainer, and a television set to watch when I was on the trainer. We've now added a mini fridge for drinks and a closet full of gear and equipment. My walls are decorated with medals and running bibs and inspirational messages, including one I painted on the wall myself: I'm not here to be average. I'm here to be awesome! This room is my sanctuary. It's where I go to prove myself to myself.

A Breast Cancer Awareness Month Interview

"The local news channel wants to do a story on you."

"A story on me? James, what are you talking about?"

"Well, with your half Ironman coming up in October, and that being Breast Cancer Awareness Month, I reached out to a couple of news channels. I thought they might want to do a story about your breast cancer and your treatments, and you training to do a half Ironman in spite of everything."

I had no idea James had done this. The thought of doing an interview terrified me! At that point in time, talking about myself and being vulnerable were not my strengths. But I had learned that personal growth only occurs when you choose to step outside your comfort zone. I had been trying to make a habit of doing things that scared me. This interview? Being on television? Those things definitely scared me!

"All right," I reluctantly agreed, "I'll do it."

Before I knew it, I had a camera crew at my house. The reporter interviewed me and James, and the crew took shots of my pain cave and of me working out. The story aired that night. It was an inspirational, feel-good piece, and they did a good job putting it together.

Word of the interview quickly got out to my coworkers, my family, and my training team. Some saw it when it aired, others saw it online, and still others pulled it up from the station archives where it currently lives.

https://www.5newsonline.com/article/news/local/springdale-athlete-training-for-ironman-race-after-battling-breast-cancer/527-5c23ae32-ac1c-4b2e-b2d8-79a82f7e8d94

I received congratulatory messages from my teammates and family members. Because I had never felt like what I was doing was a big deal, I was a bit embarrassed by the idea that I deserved any attention for it. But I realized this was my Dark Side trying to sneak in and rob me of the confidence and self-love that was building inside me as a result of my accomplishments. I had to keep reminding myself that it was a big deal. I had to keep actively shutting down those negative voices.

My First Half Ironman

James and I and some of my endurance team members arrived in Waco the Friday before the race. We wanted to acclimate to the courses and do some light training. It was cold and windy. I was already nervous, and the weather was weighing on me heavily. How was I going to get through the race when it was so cold that we barely stayed outside long enough to get registered? The lake we were going to swim in was also cold. That worried me too. I still felt anxiety during the swim portion of a race. The cold and the wind were making that anxiety ten times worse.

The day before the event, we did a short practice swim that freaked me out. The freezing water caused me to have trouble breathing. The sharp wind created waves that pounded my face. I did not even finish my five-hundred-yard swim that day. I let the elements defeat me. I gave up. The following day I would have to somehow manage to swim twenty-two hundred yards. I was not feeling confident about it, to say the least.

I was grateful that the bike course was flat and not at all intimidating. There were a few bad spots in the road, but I was now a decent cyclist so I was looking forward to this leg of the race. We biked part of the run course to get an idea of the elevation. There were three hills on the run. It was a double loop course. This meant we would have to go up each of those hills twice. I am a decent runner for my age group, usually in the top 20 to 25 percent, but I let those hills get into my head. I tried to push them out of my mind. I told myself I would deal with them when it was time.

Just when I started feeling consumed by my fears and my doubts about why I was even here, a picture arrived from the team of project managers I oversee at work. In the photo, each of them was holding up a letter. The letters spelled, "GOOD LUCK!" I've since enlarged that photo and have it hanging in my pain cave. It was just the encouragement I needed, exactly when I needed it.

The night before the race I managed to get three hours of sleep—maybe. I was going to have to run on pure adrenaline and carbohydrates.

The forecast for race day promised a cold morning with rising temperatures that would make it much warmer by the time I hit the run course. I was glad the weather was better than it had been the day before, but the water was still freezing. I was so freaked out about the swim that morning that I could not stop shaking. This was partly due to the cold, but mostly because I was reacting to the fear running through my body. To make matters worse, it was not a mass start but a rolling start. It took about an hour to get everyone into the water.

The waiting was the worst part. I heard later that they had to pull about thirty people from the water that day. The cold and other factors got the best of them. I was determined to not be one of those individuals. The moment I hit the water, I went into race mode. My fear evaporated. I had the best open water swim I ever had, exceeding my goal time by five minutes. I sighted well, stayed close to the buoys, and fought for my swim lane. There were swimmers who were swimming zig zag, swimmers who tried to pull me under or swim over me, and swimmers who would try to get my spot by the buoys. I was having none of it. I did what I was taught to do by my coach: throw elbows and kick the shit out of anyone trying to drag me down. It worked. I completed the swim without issue. Other than my hands and feet being numb when I climbed out of the water, I felt accomplished.

The bike leg is always my favorite and this course was a lot of fun. It was flat and fast, and I didn't even mind the bad roads. I was spared from getting a flat tire, and made it through the fifty-six miles with an average speed of almost 18 mph. Around the last ten miles, I did hit headwind. That significantly slowed me down. My time took a hit, but all in all, it was a seamless execution. I had enough fluid and nutrition so I did not have to stop at all during those fifty-six miles.

Along the way I saw a few wrecks, flats, and even a couple of people that were struggling with physical ailments. I was so thankful not to be one of them. Triathletes know that there are four disciplines in both the 70.3 and the 140.6 Ironman, but we never know what that fourth discipline will be until race day. It could be an injury, a mechanical issue with the bike, a wreck, mismanaging our nutrition, or something else. We must be ready for anything. That's part of the difficulty of these events.

When I started the last leg, the run, I was still feeling good. I was excited to be almost done and actually teared up at the thought of crossing that finish line on the bridge. Everything was going great until I hit the first set of hills. I ended up having to walk part of them and that messed with my head. I never really recovered from that—and from knowing I had to do those hills again on the second loop. There were parts of the run where my pace was strong and parts of the run where it was the worst it had ever been. I was getting tired and discouraged.

When I hit the hills on the second loop, I gave up for a short time. I walked them and then stopped at an aid station to get my shit together. I ate a banana, drank Red Bull, took in some salt, and psyched myself up enough to finish the run.

The last two miles were torture. I could see the bridge and hear the crowds, but I still had two miles to run to get there. I was exhausted, and my body was hurting.

Then, there it was: the bridge. At that moment, all the hurt disappeared, and I began to tear up for the second time. I saw my husband and my family cheering me on as I crossed the finish line in six hours, twenty-one minutes, and twenty-four seconds. The relief, accomplishment, and pride I felt was worth the months and months of sacrifice and suffering while training. I was halfway to my goal of completing a full 140.6 Ironman!

Even with the challenge of breast cancer, I was unstoppable.

TWENTY FIVE

Silver Linings

"Athletes' goals are attained not by strength
but by perseverance."

–Felicity Luckey

The Pandemic

The year 2020 needs no introduction. That was the year the pandemic began, life changed abruptly, races were canceled, and my dream of completing a full Ironman was put on hold. COVID-19 came out of China with a vengeance, and quickly spread to all areas of the globe. On March 11, 2020, the World Health Organization declared it a pandemic. Thousands were dying. Everyone was scared. States began shutting down. Countries shut down, and people were forced to quarantine in their homes. The world literally stopped.

As if that was not enough, 2020 was also the year that the world burned. Extreme fires raged out of control in Australia and all up and down the American west coast. President Trump decided the US should leave the Paris Climate Agreement. The unconscionable deaths of George Floyd and of too many other innocent Black people ignited riots and protests around the world. Millions mourned the passing of loved ones, while sports fans mourned the death of basketball legend Kobe Bryant and the cancellation of the 2020 Summer Olympics.

I thought my breast cancer had made 2019 a challenging year, but 2020 was something I could have never imagined. And yet, there were a few silver linings behind all those dark clouds, some positive changes that came out of the chaos. Even though there would be no races, no events, no crowds, and no training with my endurance team, I still trained every day. I had to. I would have gone crazy if I didn't have that to keep my mind and my body occupied. When the gyms, restaurants, salons, and everything else deemed non-essential were ordered to shut down, we bought a treadmill for my pain cave. My wonderful husband also bought me an Endless Pool so I could swim at home. This pool is to swimming what treadmills are to running. It takes up very little room, but has a propulsive current that basically allows you to swim in place. Now I had the full set up I needed for triathlon training—right at my own house!

While I know that working from home provided huge challenges for many people, it actually allowed me to have greater work-life balance. I enjoyed the flexibility and the opportunity it gave me to spend more time with my husband and my teenage boys. Working from home allowed me to train in the mornings, at lunch, or later in the afternoon so that my evenings were not consumed with exercising. This was definitely a bonus for my endurance sports lifestyle. Out of the ashes of 2020, I realized I was now living my best life.

Another Surgery

I had done well in my first half Ironman, placing twenty-first in my age group. But my monthly estrogen suppression shots continued to rob me of my energy. Even with my new treadmill and amazing Endless Pool, I found myself falling behind in my performance. By the summer of 2020, I could not even get through some of my workouts. My body was unable to do what I was asking of it. I was devastated that all the training, all the progress, all the improvements I had made were quickly diminishing. I was now going backward.

I am a highly competitive person with very big dreams, and this was unacceptable. I had to find another solution. Earlier in my treatment, my oncologist had suggested that having a hysterectomy might be a good option for me. He explained that removing my estrogen-producing ovaries should eliminate my need for the shots. I would just have to continue taking my daily Tamoxifen. When my doctor first mentioned this in 2019, I had a full race season ahead of me and was scheduled to do my first Ironman in 2020. With these events on my calendar, I was not willing to go through another surgery and the fight it would require to come back in my training yet again.

With the world on lockdown and my races on hold, I decided to speak to my OB about a hysterectomy. She agreed with my oncologist that this was probably the best route for me. My body was extremely strong and was not going to be forced into menopause easily. She said that having a full hysterectomy also meant not having to worry about ovarian cancer. During the pandemic, the hospital had stopped doing elective surgeries. Because of my breast cancer, this surgery was considered preventive, not elective. This allowed my doctor to squeeze me in.

I made the decision to go ahead and have the surgery. With the race season suspended, this seemed like an opportune time to move forward with a hysterectomy. I wanted to get my energy back. I was tired of fighting my body and I was tired of being tired.

Due to the pandemic, no one was allowed to come into the hospital with me. When James dropped me off, I had the passing thought that, if something went wrong during the surgery, this would be the last time I would see him.

Being in the hospital alone was not a pleasant experience. I am not one to feel lonely, but something about going through the process of surgery by myself was unsettling. I wished I had my husband beside me when I woke up. Instead, I woke up alone.

Upon waking, I was incredibly hungry, and I felt dehydrated. I was not just a little hungry and dehydrated—I drank and ate, nonstop, for hours! The volume of fluids I took in surprised the nurses, but it helped my recovery tenfold. The nurses were also surprised by how quickly I was up and moving around. They wanted me walking, so I walked, regardless of the pain. All I could think about was getting through this so I could get back to training. Because of my competitive nature, when I was walking the hall with my nurse, I was very aware of the other patients doing the same thing. I made sure to walk faster and further then anyone else on my floor. I do the same thing when I am at the gym. Running on a treadmill, the people next to me do not realize I'm racing them . . . but I am.

The other game that entertained me during my overnight stay I called, "How many times can I set off the heart rate monitor?" As an endurance athlete, my resting heart rate is very low, averaging in the mid to upper forties. I have even seen it fall below forty a time or two. Adding in the pain medication that relaxed me even more made it a real game! I totally freaked out my nurses the first couple of times the alarm went off. These machines are set somewhere in the fifties. Unless I am moving about, my heart rate is never going to be in the fifties. The nurses had to come in and manually turn off and reset the machine each time I set it off. When they learned I was an athlete and that a lower resting heart rate was normal for me, they finally conceded and just turned it off altogether. I don't know why I felt a twisted sense of pride that I beat those machines, but I did!

When I was released the next day, my one burning question was, "When can I swim, bike, and run again?" My doctor went over what I could and could not do during the week before I saw her for my follow-up visit.

This recovery process ended up being vastly different from what I experienced after my lumpectomy. With my lumpectomy, just a couple days after the surgery I was up and walking five miles. But this time, my uterus, ovaries, and everything tied to them had been cut out of my body. I had underestimated what my recovery would be like. Coming back from this surgery was much slower. I did not want to push my body and suffer a prolapse or some other setback in my recovery process.

I surprised everyone by following my doctor's orders to a tee. I was willing to do this because she worked with me on my training, outlining a plan to get me back at it as soon as possible. I could not lift anything heavy for quite some time, but as soon as my incisions healed, I was back to swimming. I was allowed to do some slow jogging and biking at three weeks. I was back to light running and biking around four weeks out. These times may not be exact, but I know for sure that I was recovering and training shockingly sooner than what others had expected. I knew I would be. I don't do well with being down.

I hated the idea of having another surgery, but it was the best option for me. I still have some serious hot flashes, and I instantly gained six to eight pounds. But I got my energy back! I could immediately tell a difference. It took me a few months to get back to where I was regarding my training, but I did get back to that performance level and have even surpassed it.

Body Image Issues Revisited

While I am pleased with my new energy levels, I am still trying to understand how I gained six to eight pounds while training for a full Ironman—and why I am not able to take it off. There is literally nothing I can do to lose that weight! I eat healthy, no dairy or meat, and train like a fiend every single day. This has been a real demon for me and has triggered my old body image issues. I am still struggling to not let this control me. I am trying to make peace with the possibility that I may never be able to get this weight off because I now have zero estrogen in my body. I turned fifty years old in the fall of 2021, and I still have to stay on top of my body image issues.

One of those old issues has to do with my feelings about swimsuits. I still wear a bikini at the age of fifty, but I'm not sure how much longer I will continue to do so. My body is beginning to look like it's fifty, and parts of me are just not staying up like they used to. Not even the amount of training I do can fight gravity!

Fortunately, I currently train with women who range in ages from the very young to older than me. One thing that helps me improve my body image is that all these women wear swimsuits confidently, no matter their age, shape, or size. This reminds me that literally no one cares what I look like. Everyone on the team, including the men, are very supportive. It's such a comfortable, non-threatening environment that I no long worry about what I'm wearing when I'm around my teammates.

This confidence helps carry me through any situation where I have to wear a swimsuit in public. Anytime I start to feel like I'm too fat, or my butt is too wrinkly, or my cellulite is showing, I remind myself that I am doing amazing things and that my body is exactly where it needs to be in the aging process. In fact, I'm actually ahead of the game because I'm a very fit middle-aged woman. I also put what I've learned about codependency to use and remind myself that, even if someone wants to judge me, what they think of me is none of my business. If they have any issue with my body, it's their issue, not mine.

TWENTY SIX

Chasing My Dream

"And here you are living despite it all."

– Rupi Kaur

Fast forward to 2021. The year of the vaccine. The year the world started to recover. The year that sporting events resumed and children returned to school. I was back in the office one or two days a week and working from home the rest of the time. I had to put up my sweats and yoga pants and get used to wearing jeans again. I had to learn how to reenter society.

Although we were not as completely isolated as some had been, my family had kept to ourselves as much as possible to try and avoid contracting COVID-19. We steered clear of group training sessions, dinners with friends, and gyms. We even put our Sunday family dinners with my mom and our adult children on hold. As an introvert, I was very comfortable in our new world. I enjoyed the isolation. Now that I was able to sit with myself and welcome the quiet around me, I actually enjoyed the forced isolation. But once our household was vaccinated, we began to reenter society, and things around us began to normalize.

The Unbreakables

In 2021, I was honored to be accepted as a member of the endurance team called "The Unbreakables." This is a team of athletes who have struggled and who may be still struggling with anything from addiction, to trauma, to injuries, or domestic abuse. These athletes have PTSD and illnesses, but they have all prevailed; they all use fitness as one way to heal and stay healthy, to achieve balance and inner serenity. Becoming a member of this team felt like coming home. There are numerous opportunities as an athlete, and a triathlete, to become an ambassador for a brand or a member of a team. None of these ever spoke to my heart the way The Unbreakables team did. We are all about sharing our stories of pain and suffering and accounts of our recovery process. The goal is to lift each other up and to inspire others.

Prior to writing this book, and the motivational speaking I do now, being vulnerable did not come easy to me. I enjoyed talking to others about their personal experiences and trying to help in any manner I could. But even after Hoffman, with the exception of my husband, I still tended to not share or burden others with my feelings. I just didn't trust that others wouldn't reject me because of my experiences. I still carried a small pocket of shame.

The Unbreakables helped me move beyond all this. With them, I was able to share the good days and the bad without fear of rejection or judgement. There are many on the team with whom I felt an instant connection. Everyone on this team has a back story.

Each of us has a tattered past. I felt comfortable sharing because I knew these individuals were kindred spirits.

Becoming part of The Unbreakables allowed me to take more steps on my journey of self-healing. It provided me with more solid bricks for rebuilding my self-esteem. This team provided me with a safe space and with an opportunity to get my story out so it can motivate and provide hope for others; so it can inspire people to believe in and love themselves.

My College Diploma

On March 22, 2021, I received my diploma in the mail: a Bachelor's degree in Business Administration with a concentration in Project Management. I had begun working online to obtain my degree more than ten years earlier, when I was still married to Mike. It had been a requirement for me to move into a management position. My boss had told me, "As long as you are working on it, it doesn't matter how long it takes." He knew I had a heavy load, both at work and at home. I appreciated that he was always willing to work with me.

I never gave this piece of paper much thought, other than it was a requirement for my job. But when I received my diploma in the mail, I got emotional. I was not emotional when I finished my last class. I was not emotional when I found out my GPA was 3.85. I was not emotional when my boss leaked this information to the team I manage and they made me a medal. Honestly, I was embarrassed that it took me ten years to get my bachelor's degree. This was my primary feeling about the whole thing. And I felt relief—relief that I could finally lay down this burden of continual classwork. But I was not emotional. It wasn't until I saw the actual diploma, with my name, and the words Magna Cum Laude, that I teared up. That's when I got emotional.

The first thing I did was show my husband. The second thing I did was take a picture and post it on the The Unbreakables' Facebook page. My husband and The Unbreakables would understand how much this meant. They would understand the challenges and the perseverance it took to accomplish this. They would understand why it took me so long. The sheer tenacity required to keep pushing through all those years was exhausting, but it finally paid off.

Once again, I had proven to myself that I could do hard things. I had made another dream come true.

TWENTY SEVEN

What It Takes

"You can keep going and your legs might hurt for a week,
or you can quit and your mind will hurt for a lifetime."

--Mark Allen

One hundred and forty point six miles (140.6). That's what our bodies must carry us through to complete a full Ironman. It takes months, even a year or more of grueling training and race preparation to cross an Ironman finish line in the allotted amount of time—seventeen hours. It takes even more than the blood, sweat, and tears that literally seep from our pores on a daily basis. Completing an endurance event like this takes an incredible amount of mental strength and grit, not only on race day, but every day we train.

Triathletes can choose to train ourselves by finding a training plan online, or we can opt to have a coach work with us and provide those daily training plans. I like to have a coach to work with for the accountability. Besides, I just don't have time to create my own schedules and ensure that I am getting the most out of myself. I need someone to push me, to provide just the right workouts so as to not burn me out, but to work me hard enough that I'll see progress year after year. This is a hobby for me, but it is also my lifestyle—my passion. I want to qualify for the World Championships someday, and I know I am more likely to get there with a coach.

My typical week consists of eighteen- to twenty-hours of training that includes a mix of cycling, swimming, running and strength training. Each day is different, and the schedule ebbs and flows. There are recovery weeks where the time and intensity are much lighter. Closer to the event, the weeks are more intense. Rarely do I have a day off from training, so it's basically seven days a week. The week before the race is what we refer to as a "taper" week. The training is very light, so much so that it's common for athletes to get restless and anxious.

One of the greatest challenges of committing to a full Ironman event is finding the balance between work, family, and training. It requires sacrifice. It demands commitment from both the athlete and their family. I am very fortunate to have had the full support of my husband and my children ever since I started my endurance sports training back in 2017. Back then, my oldest son had already left home, and my daughter was in high school. She and James pitched in and were especially helpful in making sure my two sons, who were almost out of elementary school, got to all of their events.

Even though the COVID-19 lockdown has ended, I am still working from home several days a week. That makes it easier for me to schedule my training than if I was going into the office every day. It's common for me to train on my lunch break and then jump on a meeting. After a lunch hour in my Endless Pool, I have been known to show up to a virtual meeting sporting "swim goggle eyes." Most coworkers that know me don't even think twice about it anymore. They've gotten used to it. They are even a bit intrigued by what I do every day.

Along with doing our actual workouts, triathletes must also learn the rules for each event. Every race has an Athlete Guide which outlines the schedule for the day, what the courses look like, transition areas, and the rules. Even though the rules are primarily the same, different locations do have different logistics. That's why I spend hours and hours meticulously reviewing the guide for each event. I confirm the drafting policy (meaning how close you can be to other riders), how to pass properly without a time penalty, and rules for littering and drop zones. The guide breaks down the time cutoffs for each discipline, as well as the start time, that is, whether or not the swimmers will start all at once or in waves. It breaks down how many gear bags triathletes will have, how to body mark, and how to label our bike and bike helmet. There are rules about what we can and cannot wear and how warm the water must be to ditch the wetsuit. There are even rules about what kinds of wetsuits are legal. For a planner like myself, the information can be dizzying! When I race triathlons, regardless of the distance, I am more stressed out by the logistics of the day than I am by the actual race. To feel confident, I start studying the guide at least a month out.

Part of the logistics for a particular event involve coordinating multiple gear bags and preparing for transition points. A transition point is where we have gear bags staged after each discipline so we can change and fuel before moving to the next leg of the race. We must have the proper gear and even the ability to do minor adjustments on our bike. We need to mentally practice moving through each transition by picturing it in our heads to ensure we don't forget anything. We must be able to move through it quickly so as to not eat up precious time.

Nutrition and hydration are key. If we do not manage our fluid and calorie intake, it could be disastrous. Nailing our hydration and nutrition during long events takes practice. It can be a bit of a trial-and-error process. Our bodies are all different, and our systems react differently to how and when we take in solids and liquids, and even to which ones we ingest. For example, I don't like eating solid food on the run, for fear of choking, so I have found that using gels works best for me. I also drink liquid nutrition just to make sure I'm getting enough calories at the end. The bike leg is another story. I treat it like a rolling buffet. I have my watch set to beep every thirty minutes to remind me to eat and every ten minutes to drink. I pack my bento bag with fig newtons, miniature Pay Day candy bars, energy gummies, and Crustable sandwiches. I tend to overeat on the bike. Since I have mastered the art of eating while cycling, it's easy to pack in the calories. But if I'm well fueled going into the run, there's less chance of me running out of steam, even if I am not perfect with my nutrition on that last leg. One of the most important aspects of fueling is to make sure we take in enough salt, especially if it's hot out. That can be accomplished by sucking on tablets, electrolyte drinks, or even carrying a small tube of powder to dip into when needed. I rely on the dissolvable tablets and drink mixes. I will even drop a tablet or two into my drink mixes in the summer months when the heat is extreme.

Panic!

The triathlon community has a running joke about "wrapping yourself in bubble wrap" leading up to a big race. Since athletes can train for months, or even a year, for just one race, the last thing we want is to have a race-ending illness or injury right before the big event. This almost happened to me in 2021, just two weeks out from Ironman Tulsa, my first full 140.6 event.

One evening, while sitting on the couch watching TV with my husband, I started to feel a pain in my side. It was a constant, nagging pain, kind of on my side but also kind of near my stomach. My mind immediately began to think about all the organs and muscles that were located in the vicinity that was hurting. I'd had some issues with my upper colon earlier in the year. My initial thought was that maybe this issue was back. Then it occurred to me that the pain was not located anywhere near my small or large intestines. As the pain continued, and even increased, I began to panic.

In my frantic state, I did what every rational human being does when presented with this situation; I turned to Google for advice. After plugging in my symptoms, I quickly came up with another cause for my pain: I had appendicitis. I was certain of it—so certain that I began to tear up. I instantly began mourning the loss of my race and all the hard work and countless hours of training and preparation I had put into it. As I sat down to tell my husband that

I needed another surgery and that my dreams were shattered again, I could not hold back the tears.

James listened calmly. Then he took control of the situation, asking questions about the location and severity of my pain.

"Where is your pain?" I pointed to my side because the pain had gone from just a generalized annoyance to a more isolated spot along my side. James pointed out that appendicitis pain is typically more in the front, around the belly button. That did not deter me because I had already made up my mind that an organ had exploded inside of me and I needed immediate medical attention.

"Are you running a fever?" Well, no I wasn't. But my body is extremely resilient, so that explained that.

"Does it hurt to touch?"

"No, but it hurts to move. That's kind of the same thing."

It only took my husband about three minutes to rule out appendicitis and somewhat put my mind at ease. I am so grateful that he was able to rationally assess the situation because my brain had already disappeared down the rabbit hole. If he had not been there, I would have already been in my car and on the way to the emergency room.

Okay, so I probably didn't need surgery. Feeling massive relief, I began to calm down. I went back to Google and started researching again. Now that the discomfort was more localized, I realized it might be a pulled muscle in my oblique area. I researched the topic "strained oblique" and found out that all my symptoms matched. I initially thought I must have pulled it swimming, but after reevaluation, I realized I do not swim fast enough to hurt myself. I have only one speed and that is "sloth."

I retraced my activities over the last several days to try and pinpoint how the injury could have occurred. Then I remembered that my Endless Pool has a lid—a very heavy lid. When I lift the sides of the pool cover, I am reaching up. Lifting the first side is extra difficult because the suction must be broken. The light bulb finally went off. I pulled my oblique muscle lifting my Endless Pool lid to go for a swim!

Welcome to being almost fifty years old!

My brief feeling of relief turned into panic again as I thought, "How am I going to swim 2.4 miles with a strained oblique muscle?" I literally need that muscle just for swimming. Over the next couple of days, I did not train. Instead, I hit that muscle with everything I could throw at it—ice, ibuprofen, and a heating pad. I even kept it taped up with kinesiology tape. The purpose of taping up my side was to restrict the movement of the muscle and support it while it healed. My coach instructed me to keep it taped up moving forward and throughout the Ironman.

Fortunately, this story had a happy ending. My oblique muscle healed. When it was time to race the Ironman, it was merely a whisper of slight discomfort. I was back in the game, Baby!

TWENTY EIGHT

My First Ironman 140.6

*"Strength grows in the moments when you think
you can't go on, but you keep going anyway."*
–Karen Salmansohn

Glow Sticks

When I was a kid hanging out at the roller rinks, glow sticks were a welcome sight. You absolutely had to have one when they were handed out! The lights at the rink would be turned off, and we'd hang those glow sticks all over our bodies. We thought they were cool, and we thought we were cool when we got them.

As the sun sets over the Ironman Tulsa 140.6 course, the volunteers start handing out glow sticks to the runners. I do not feel like one of the cool kids now. This glow stick tells me that I am in the back of the pack, that I am in jeopardy of not making the seventeen-hour cutoff. I feel like spectators watching me shuffle by are thinking, "Bless her heart. I hope she makes it." Most likely, that is not the case at all. It is probably all in my head. Undoubtedly, it is my Dark Side coming for me.

My body is wracked with pain. Every step I take jars me to my core. My mind goes back to obsessing over the glow sticks. I cannot let go of the damn glow sticks! Why does it upset me so much to be out here in the dark? Just being brave enough to attempt such a feat is courageous. Why am I so hard on myself?

I know these are my abusers' voices sitting on my shoulder, taunting me, whispering in my ear that just being out here is not good enough. I have to do better. I have to be competitive. I have to meet my race goals. When the glow sticks come out at the aid stations, my Dark Side reminds me that I am one step closer to the sweepers removing me from the course because I have no chance of making the required cutoff time.

Having a glow stick handed to me is a painful reminder of just how badly the entire day has gone.

Go Time!

The hotel alarm clock went off at 2:00 a.m. on the big day, May 23, 2021. Time to get up, eat breakfast, drink a shit ton of caffeine, and get dressed.

I had gone to bed at 7:30 the night before, but my body just didn't understand what was happening. I laid awake most of the night, trying to calm my mind, but mostly obsessing over the upcoming race. I mentally rehearsed my goals and my plans for each transition. I don't think I got more than three hours of sleep. Adrenaline and caffeine would have to carry me through, and I figured I was in good company. I was certain that everyone racing was feeling the same and that even the professional athletes were not exempt from pre-race anxiety.

Surprisingly, I wasn't a total disaster on race morning. I managed to eat some oatmeal with a banana and down lots of coffee. I had all my gear methodically planned and laid out the day before, so there was no last-minute rush to gather my items. My thoughts were the only thing that needed to be corralled.

James was tasked with dropping me off at the shuttles at 4:00 a.m. The traffic patterns for getting approximately three thousand race participants there had not been well thought out. Lines of cars had come to a complete standstill trying to get to the university where the shuttles waited. Impatient athletes began pouring out of the cars, choosing to walk the last half mile. I was one of them. With a quicker "Goodbye!" to James than I had hoped for, I grabbed my three gear bags and joined the march. It was still dark and rainy, but there was a nervous excitement in the air.

I was ecstatic to be a part of it all. Throughout the morning, I was frequently delighted by the surreal thought, "I am going to do an Ironman today!" After two years of preparation, battling cancer and a pandemic and recovering from a hysterectomy, I was here. I had to fight like hell to make it, but I was here.

The bus was full of anxious athletes. Due to COVID-19, we all had to wear masks. I don't know if it was because we had cloth covering our mouths, or because everyone was trying to meditate and prepare their mind for what was coming, but there was an eerie silence throughout the duration of our twenty-minute ride. The sun had not yet come out, so the blackness of the early morning only magnified the eeriness.

After my own failed attempt at breathing exercises and meditation, I began to look around. I was curious to see what other athletes were doing. Some had their heads back and their eyes closed, maybe meditating, maybe sleeping. Some had their heads hanging forward or against the seat, eyes also closed. There were a few quietly chatting with each other, but not many. Some were just gazing out into the darkness through the window. I heard one say a quick prayer.

When we arrived at our destination, we learned that we were not yet done with our hike. After setting up our first transition area with whatever we needed on the bike leg, we would have to walk a mile to the swim start. Today's 141 miles just became 142 miles! I was hoping that these miles did not continue to add up as I was already questioning my ability to do the original 140.6.

I enjoyed the walk to the lake. It was quite comforting because it gave me time to take deep breaths and practice some positive mantras.

"You can do this."

"You can do hard things."

"You are a shark." (I always use this shark mantra to psyche myself up for the swim.)

As these affirmations circled through my thoughts, I giggled to myself as I whispered under my breath, "Dead men walking." It was a morbid thought, but the hundreds of athletes slowly moving in a line, coupled with the eerie quietness, reminded me of the death row marches I had seen in movies. The few athletes within ear shot did not appreciate my dark humor. They shot me looks implying, "I cannot believe you just said that." I found their responses amusing, which helped ease the tension souring through my body. This made it worth the disparaging looks.

All the athletes were carrying their gear bags, and most carried their wetsuits since it would have been dreadfully hot to walk that distance wearing them. Without much conversation, we made our way close to the swim chutes. The line scattered at this point. We each found a spot where we could put on our wetsuit, swim cap, and goggles and make sure we were ready to get in the water. Managing to find some of my teammates further helped calm my nerves. They were all strong swimmers, and I doubted they felt the anxiety about the swim that I was feeling.

My swim anxiety was not as bad as it used to be, but it was still there. I was keenly aware that athletes died every year participating in these Ironman events, and it's almost always in the swim portion of the race. My hope is that someday my swimming will be strong enough that I'll feel as confident about this leg as I feel about the bike and the run. That's my goal. But that day, my head was still running the show in the water.

A Debilitating First Leg

We had to line up in chutes in preparation for a few of us being released about three to five seconds apart. Because of COVID-19, the idea was to keep everyone distanced as much as possible. It did not take long for swimmers to bunch up out in the water, even with the attempt at spacing us. Waiting for my turn to enter the lake on race morning, I experienced a range of emotions: happiness, anxiety, nervousness, fear, and even relief. Once I hit the water and find my rhythm, the swim anxiety usually dissipates. I get into a nice, smooth tempo and focus on sighting the buoys to help guide me. Focusing on the buoys also keeps my mind occupied while I tell myself to just get to one buoy at a time. Just keep swimming.

While standing among the other edgy swimmers, I quickly realized that I had made a grave error by only bringing my mirrored swim goggles. Sighting the yellow buoys with a cloudy, overcast sky would have been difficult enough. But it was also raining. My mirrored goggles are meant for sunny weather. I realized my error could cost me a significant amount of time in the water. The forecast predicted rain for a good portion of the event, depending on how quickly one could complete it. Knowing my usual pace, I estimated that I would be racing in the rain up until at least the last half of the bike leg. This made me more tense because I knew the roads were rough and there were hills. Lots of hills. I was already stressing about the bike leg and I hadn't even hit the water yet!

This was the other grave error I made that day; I let my Dark Side in before my race even began.

When I plunged into the water, I was pleasantly surprised that it did not feel all that cold. Our lake at home was ten degrees cooler, so I was well prepared for the temperature of this swim. But right away, I had issues seeing out of my mirrored goggles. I struggled staying on course the entire swim. I remember thinking, "Why does this feel like it's taking forever?" Now I know why. Due to my sighting challenges, I swam 4,993 yards instead of the approximately 4,200 required yards!

To make matters worse, I incurred an injury. Around the first thousand yards, a large man swam over me, kicking me square in the face. This was not uncommon in these races. The swim in a triathlon is actually called the "washing machine," due to the jumbled cluster of swimmers, the thrashing and kicking of bodies, and the fight to find a lane and be close to the buoys. Stronger swimmers literally swim on top of the weaker ones and that is why, for many of us, it is the most intimidating and dreaded leg of the race. I'm used to the chaos in the water, but this kick caught me off guard. The man's foot hit in such a way that my goggles were kicked out of place and I went under. My nose, mouth, and goggles immediately filled with water.

When I came up for air, I had a hard time expelling the water and getting my bearings. My nose was bleeding slightly. As I re-adjusted my goggles, it must have been apparent I was in distress. A safety kayaker came alongside to see if I needed assistance. I felt I could manage on my own, so I yelled, "No," and waved him away. The adrenaline was pumping hard through my body so I felt no pain. I had to stop three more times to adjust my goggles so they wouldn't leak. That whole incident ate up at least another ten minutes of precious time. Between this mishap and the extra yards I had swum unnecessarily, I finished thirty minutes slower than I should have on the swim.

When I finally made it to the end of that leg and saw how long it had taken me, I was crushed. My dreams of qualifying for Kona in this race were left behind in the water, along with my ego and, literally, a bit of my blood, sweat and tears. I knew at this point that I just needed to survive the day and cross that finish line. I was sad, but mostly I was angry at myself.

I hobbled out of the water, dazed from being in the lake for almost two hours. Attempting to climb the steeply inclined boat ramp, I immediately felt ill. Dizzy and nauseous, I struggled to get my wetsuit off. I had never felt sick coming off a swim before, so this made me even angrier. I still had to find my bike amongst the thousands staged in the transition area, change into my biking gear, walk up another slope to get out on the course, and mount my bike.

I sat down at my transition spot and dug through my bike gear bag for something to eat. Knowing how hungry I would be after that long swim, I had wisely packed snacks and a drink. I wanted to start the bike leg well fueled. I did not want to spare the time it would take to wait until the nausea disappeared, so I did the things I needed to do as best I could, even though I still felt dizzy and sick. My cleated bike shoes were slippery to walk in, and the rain was certainly not helping matters. Making my way up to the mount line as quickly as I could, I prayed I wouldn't have a wreck feeling the way I did.

Rain, Potholes, Flats, and Wrecks

When I clip into my bike, I am usually filled with a sense of relief and excitement. The swim is behind me and the bike is my strongest discipline. I know I can make up time here, and I love the feeling of racing on my bike. Especially this bike. This is my third bike designed just for the sport of triathlon. It is the equivalent of a Porsche in the world of cars. This bike is like riding a rocket; I was ready to assume the aero position and move into beast mode.

My joy quickly diminished as the rain continued to pound the riders. I was using a tinted visor for this leg of the race as well, so I was having the same difficulty seeing in the rain as I had suffered

during the swim. To make matters worse, the roads were not con-
ducive for fast racing on a stiff and technical race bike. Throughout the 112 miles, I rarely felt the joy I had hoped to experience.
I was seldom in a position where I could truly push the limits of
my new bike.

The first time I saw James since he dropped me off near the
shuttle was right after I came out of that first transition area. He
was yelling and waving and so excited to see me! I was on my
bike, but still feeling dizzy and nauseous from the swim. I was
fresh with emotions from the horrid time I'd had in the water. Giv-
en all this—and the fact that it was still pouring rain—I was not in
a good head space. I gave a half-hearted wave, feeling even more
upset with myself, disappointed that I couldn't muster a greater
show of appreciation for his support.

What I didn't find out until after the race was that James' exu-
berance had to do with the fact that seeing me dispelled his fears
that I had drowned or that something awful had happened to me.
My swim time was way over what it should have been, and no
one had seen me come out of the water. James was so concerned
that I had not appeared when I should have that he had a sheriff
try to get information on me. To make things worse, the tracking
application that spectators were using showed me stopping at the
end of the swim for almost thirty minutes. It was some sort of
glitch that eventually resolved itself, but the timing of the glitch
heightened my husband's distress. When he heard an ambulance
being called to the boat dock, James panicked, thinking it was
being summoned for me. He told me later that he thought, "After
everything Meredith has survived, it's the Ironman that's going to

kill her." That's why he was watching for me right at the beginning of the bike course and why he could not contain his joy upon seeing me.

Even though I may not have shown it at the time, seeing him standing there and cheering me on made all the difference in the world. It gave me motivation to fight through the rain and the poor conditions and to not give up—even though I already felt somewhat defeated.

My body did not begin to settle down and regulate until after the first couple of miles. It was still pouring down rain, and I still struggled to see through my tinted visor. My coach told me he ended up tossing his during the ride and going without. "Brilliant!" I thought. "That's what I should have done." It would have cost me sixty dollars to replace it, but that would have been well worth it.

Because I had not yet purchased a bike computer, I was relying on my watch for my metrics. With my aging eyes, my watch is already difficult to see. The rain made it practically impossible. I could not see my wattage and at times I could barely make out the mph. Watts measure how hard I am working on the bike. Being able to monitor my wattage is important so I don't overdo it on the bike section and zap my legs for the run. With poor visibility, I couldn't tell if I was utilizing my watts properly. Basically, I just hunkered down and tried to survive 112 miles of hills, rain, and roads that looked like they had been chewed up by angry giants.

The running joke after the event was that you could basically build a bike from the pieces littering the route. Water bottles, cages, random bike parts, and even a seat were seen throughout the day. It was like the Hunger Games out there. It was going to be survival of the fittest—and the best maintained bike.

I knew that, somewhere in the first fifteen miles, the road had a sharp decline coupled with a long section full of potholes and gravel. I was aware of this area because James and I had attempted to bike the course as a training session awhile back. We didn't even get twelve miles because this section took us out. The extremely bumpy conditions rattled my husband's water bottle and tire repair kit off his bike. They lay somewhere along the roadside. James was not willing to go back and hunt for these items because, around the area where he lost them, we had encountered a German Shepherd. This dog loved to terrorize cyclists! It ran my husband off the road, into the grass, and cornered him. I stopped, panicked because I thought James was being mauled by this beast. We both yelled at the dog and threatened it with a stick until James could get going on his bike again. While grateful that he was not attacked, that was it for us. Our day was done.

So here I was, once again having to take on this dreaded section fraught with beast and gravel. At least I was prepared for it. When I came to the hill, I rode the hell out of my brakes. I was not only trying to keep watch for potholes through the rain, but I was also looking for that German Shephard. The dog was nowhere to be found. Maybe he chased the professionals earlier in the day and tired of the game. Maybe his owner kept him inside on race days. Whatever the reason, I was grateful for his absence. Now I just had to contend with this descent down Satan's slide.

Due to the rain and the fact that my bike and I were completely saturated, my disc brakes screamed all the way down that hill. Passing me, a friendly cyclist yelled out, "I hear ya sister!" The god-awful squealing of my brakes and his comment made me giggle. I forgot, just for a moment, how miserable that hill was. At the bottom, I saw an ambulance and another rescue vehicle. My heart went out to that athlete. I hoped they were not too badly injured.

There were a few wrecks in that section during the day, but I was not one of them. Because the road conditions were slick, rough, and dangerous, and we were not separated from traffic for a good part of the bike ride, I made the conscious decision, early in the bike leg, to hold back and be extremely cautious. After the race, I learned that approximately two hundred sixty flat tires had to be attended to that day, and numerous athletes had experienced bike wrecks, including two professionals. Two other athletes were struck by vehicles. I knew my decision to be extra cautious would result in me finishing with an even slower time, but I felt it was better than not finishing at all due to a wreck, a flat, or mechanical issues. I'm glad I made that decision.

The Marathon Shuffle

As I approached the second transition area, I was not completely trashed, but I was questioning how I was now supposed to run 26.2 miles. The stress, the weather, and the tough conditions of the day had worn on me, and I was fatigued. I had already swum almost three miles and biked 112. The remaining 26.2 miles seemed unachievable to me. I tried to push the negative thoughts out of my head and focus on one mile at a time.

During my 112-mile bike ride, I thought I was moving quicker than I was. So again, I was deeply disappointed when I saw my final time for this leg. I was not yet in jeopardy of missing the run cutoff, but I was missing my goals by quite a bit. I stowed my bike and sat on the wet pavement to take off my bike gear and put on my running gear. It felt good to be off the bike. I was looking forward to just running and to not having the fear of drowning or wrecking looming over me. Now it was just me and my legs.

Coming out of that transition, I saw my husband, my daughter, and the young man she had married in 2019. That lifted my spirits. I even managed a smile and a quick exchange of words as I hobbled past them. As I forced my legs to go from a fast walk to a slow run, I was surprised that it was not horrible . . . yet.

The sun never appeared that day, which was a blessing, but on the one part of this course where I wanted the cool rain to hit me, it did not. The rain stopped right after I began my run, making it muggy and humid. I knew I could not run at a normal marathon race pace if I was going to survive 26 miles. I had to start slow and keep the pace more manageable. I ran the first thirteen to fourteen miles under an eleven-minute-per-mile pace. I was happy with this. I was under no illusions that I would come out and kill the run, but I did hope to run as much of it as possible.

My plan was to stop every mile for fluids instead of carrying my own hydration. I did not stop at the aid stations for long, maybe thirty seconds at first. Just long enough to get the water, the Gatorade and the Red Bull down me. I also took the opportunity to use the porta potty whenever I had to go to the bathroom. In the swim and on my bike, I freely peed on myself. Stopping was either not an option or just too much of a hassle, too time consuming. The porta potties were a welcome break for me, especially during the second half of the run.

Halfway through the marathon, I was still clicking along in

fairly good spirits. Shortly after that, my body decided it had gone far enough for one day. It began to remind me that I was almost fifty years old. My right knee, the one I always keep braced, started hurting more and more. My feet ached terribly. My legs hurt from top to bottom and my left calf kept seizing up on me. Now, my thirty-second breaks at the aid stations turned into sixty- to ninety-second breaks because I also had to stretch out my calves. I knew my time was slipping away with each mile. Even though I saw some of my teammates on the run, it did not motivate me. Knowing I was behind all of them was a difficult pill to swallow.

From the very beginning of the day, I had struggled to keep my Dark Side in check, especially after my disappointing swim and discouraging bike time. But after the halfway point of the run, I didn't have the mental energy to fight it any longer. I allowed my Dark Side to consume me, and my mind ran the rest of the day. The last twelve miles were ugly. It hurt to move my body, but I was angry with myself for not pushing through the pain and running more to make up some time. I hated that my mind was winning.

At mile seventeen, I am handed that damn glow stick. Another mile, and I succumb to the dishonor of wrapping it through my running belt.

Mile nineteen. I see my family, but I feel defeated. Approaching my husband, the second round of tears fall. All I want, more than anything in the world, is a hug. James gives me that hug, and out of my mouth come the words that are my biggest fear, "I don't think I'm going to make the cutoff. I don't think I can do this."

I still have seven miles left to go. I am exhausted. Every cell in my body hurts. I am angry with myself for performing so poorly. I want to quit. I want a shower, a bed, and food with some substance to it.

James steps back, grabs my shoulders, and looks me right in the eyes. "You are the strongest person I know. You can do this. Just keep moving forward. You did not come this far to quit. Just walk fast if you have to, but you are not quitting."

James' tough love is working. I am moving forward. I jog as much as I can.

I hear a spectator say to me, "Forward is a pace." I grab on to that mantra too.

"You are not quitting."

"Forward is a pace."

"You are not quitting."

"Forward is a pace."

With these words ringing in my ears, somehow my body covers the last brutal miles.

Mile twenty-five. I hear the crowd cheering and the cow bells ringing. The announcer is calling the names of those that are finishing their Ironman journey. Inspired, I start running again. The thought of my name being called sends goosebumps across my entire body. I am going to make it! I am going to be an Ironman!

I am the only person in the group of athletes around me who is actually running by this point. Someone behind me calls out, "Good for you!" I refuse to walk across the finish line. I always sprint my finish lines and this is not going to be any different.

As I head down the coveted red carpet lining the chute towards the timing mat, I begin to sprint. My competitive self wants to pass the gentleman directly in front of me and the lady in front of him before we cross the timing mat. I pass the gentlemen and hear one of the spectators call to him, "You just got chicked!" I feel proud of myself. I need that small win, even if it is miniscule. I sprint past the lady. Again, I feel accomplished.

Then it happens. I hear my name called out, "Meredith Thornton, you are an Ironman!"

I begin to cry as the realization of what I just accomplished sets in. My husband, daughter, and son-in-law are here waiting for me, hugging me. As they cover me with the traditional aluminum blanket, I collapse in James' arms and continue to cry. Feelings of nausea and dizziness overtake me. I lay down right there on the curb. My body has done all it needed to do today, and it is done.

* * * * * * * * * * * * * *

On May 23, 2021, I became an Ironman. I completed a grueling 2.4-mile swim, 112-mile bike ride, and 26.2-mile run in fifteen hours, twenty-six minutes, and five seconds (15:26:5). Completing my first Ironman was a massive achievement. Yet, my time was not what I had hoped for or anticipated.

While my abilities were not best showcased on this day, what was on display was my grit and my refusal to quit. No matter how frustrated I was over my time splits, the weather, and how much pain my body was in, I refused to accept defeat. My Dark Side kept telling me I was not going to make the time cutoff. It kept trying to convince me that my body would not hold out. But just as I have my entire life, I kept fighting. I fought for every single mile. I fought for my medal, and I fought for the finish line.

What I was really fighting for was for every person out there who has ever been made to feel "less than." I was fighting for any person that is currently questioning their self-worth, questioning if they are lovable, questioning if they can do hard things. I needed to accomplish this goal so I could prove to myself, and to anyone who doesn't believe in themselves, that we can do anything we put our minds to. We must never allow anyone or anything to set limits on us.

Iron Will

I am a mother, a wife, a sister, and a daughter. I have cheated death multiple times and survived traumatic injuries and illnesses. I have suffered through childhood abuse, negative body image, domestic violence, and breast cancer. And here I am—living in spite of it all. Not just living, but thriving! I am an athlete, an endurance athlete, and a triathlete. I am a 70.3 Ironman finisher, and I am an Ironman.

To my Dark Side and my abusers I say, "You gave me broken bricks throughout my childhood and into adulthood. But I have worked hard. I have replaced those cracked, crumbling bricks with self-love, self-worth, and a commitment to my well-being. Tell me now that I am not worthy. Try to tell me now that I am not enough. You told me I can't do hard things. Really?! You're a liar. You've always been a liar. I am part of the 0.01 percent of people that have completed a full Ironman. That is a very exclusive number."

One of the first things my daughter asked me when I finished Tulsa was, "What are you going to do now, Mom?"

My response, "Keep doing these races and get faster."

I have not fulfilled my dreams with just one Ironman. I want to go to the big show. I want to race in the Kona World Championships. Two weeks later I signed up for my next Ironman because I am not yet done with my story.

In a lot of ways, I'm just beginning.

EPILOGUE

In October of 2021, five months after doing Tulsa, I completed my second full Ironman. Finding a coach whom I knew could get me closer to the podium, I poured my whole soul into training. I improved my time by an hour and a half, completing Ironman Waco in thirteen hours, fifty-three minutes, and twenty-five seconds (13:53:25). I placed tenth in my age group.

I missed the podium by five spots. But given that I placed forty-seventh in my age group in Tulsa, I am satisfied with these results. They give me confidence that, one day, I will indeed get into the top five in my age group, which will qualify me for the World Championships. I almost gave up on that dream after my shaky performance in Tulsa, but I didn't. That is why we must never give up. The only sure way to fail is to not even try.

In April 2022, I received a text that brought me even greater happiness than my second Ironman results. It was from my oldest son. After so many years of him not wanting to have any contact with me, he finally reached out. I was overwhelmed with joy and did not hesitate to connect with him. I am so thankful to have my first-born back in my life, and to have an opportunity to get to know his children, my grandchildren.

For me, this is another miracle. This is another indicator that my guardian angel is still looking out for me—and I am grateful.

Meredith's **"I Can Do Hard Things"** Goal for 2023:

Standing on top of Mt. Kilimanjaro

ACCOMPLISHED!

CONTACT MEREDITH

If you would like to write to the author, or have her speak to your group or organization, please contact Meredith at:
mathornton23@yahoo.com

www.ingramcontent.com/pod-product-compliance
Lightning Source LLC
Chambersburg PA
CBHW060909120626
46553CB00001B/259